DEVIL'S ADVOCATES

DEVIL'S ADVOCATES is a series of books devoted to exploring the classics of horror cinema. Contributors to the series come from the fields of teaching, academia, journalism and fiction, but all have one thing in common: a passion for the horror film and a desire to share it with the widest possible audience.

'The admirable Devil's Advocates series is not only essential – and fun – reading for the serious horror fan but should be set texts on any genre course.'
Dr Ian Hunter, Professor of Film Studies, De Montfort University, Leicester

'Auteur Publishing's new Devil's Advocates critiques on individual titles... offer bracingly fresh perspectives from passionate writers. The series will perfectly complement the BFI archive volumes.' **Christopher Fowler, *Independent on Sunday***

'Devil's Advocates has proven itself more than capable of producing impassioned, intelligent analyses of genre cinema... quickly becoming the go-to guys for intelligent, easily digestible film criticism.' ***Horror Talk.com***

'Auteur Publishing continue the good work of giving serious critical attention to significant horror films.' ***Black Static***

 DevilsAdvocatesbooks

DevilsAdBooks

DEVIL'S ADVOCATES

IT FOLLOWS

JOSHUA GRIMM

Acknowledgments

First and foremost, thanks to the indispensable John Atkinson at Auteur for his guidance, patience and insight. I also appreciate the Manship School of Mass Communication at Louisiana State University for providing the time, resources, and support to complete this manuscript, and my colleagues for their helpful suggestions and advice. Thanks to Dr. Paul Eisenstein for teaching me about film criticism and appreciation, and for providing the template for what a professor should be. I'm lucky to have friends constantly offering their unwavering support and encouragement, be it from hundreds of miles away or just down the hall. Of them, this time I'll single out Jared, who served as my horror movie consultant on this project and in life. Of course, thanks to my incredible parents, Randy and Carolyn, who have only ever encouraged me to follow my dreams, whatever they may be at that moment. Thank you to my son, Jack, for sleeping just long enough during his first months so that I could submit the first draft. And most of all, thank you to my amazing wife, Claire – our annual horror movie marathons during Shocktember and Rocktober are highlights in an already-perfect life.

First published in 2018 by
Auteur, 24 Hartwell Crescent, Leighton Buzzard LU7 1NP
www.auteur.co.uk
Copyright © Auteur 2018

Series design: Nikki Hamlett at Cassels Design
Set by Cassels Design www.casselsdesign.co.uk

British Library Cataloguing-in-Publication Data
A catalogue record for this book is available from the British Library

ISBN paperback: 978-1-911325-58-1
ISBN ebook: 978-1-911325-59-8

CONTENTS

INTRODUCTION

Around the age of 10, director David Robert Mitchell had a recurring nightmare of being slowly followed by something that could adopt multiple identities. Regardless of how many times he escaped, no matter how often he evaded capture, it just kept following. Roughly three decades later, his film *It Follows* (2015) premiered at Cannes, where it was a breakout hit; it went on to become a critical success. Pulling a robust 97% on Rotten Tomatoes, *It Follows* was hailed as a 'teen movie you've never seen before', a 'creepy, mesmerizing exercise in minimalist horror', 'the best horror film in years', and simply, 'so damn good'. Along with the critical accolades, the film was a financial success as well. Taking advantage of Michigan's tax credits, *It Follows* was made for a paltry $1.3 million, grossing nearly 17 times that at the box office worldwide. In an unprecedented strategy, the film itself was supposed to be released on VOD two weeks after opening in theatres; following the film's success, the VOD timeline had to be moved back, something slyly permitted in the contract.[1]

Along with being profitable, *It Follows* also joined a horror movie renaissance of smart, frightening films that have rejuvenated the genre. Following *Scream* (1996) and *The Blair Witch Project* (1999), horror movies were bogged down by the success of Japanese remakes and torture flicks in the early noughties, followed by an unrelenting march of the supernatural both in film and television. The genre was far from dead—the era saw the release of the bloody, brilliant (and bloody brilliant) film *The Descent* (2005), one of the all-time greats—as an entire genre simply doesn't disappear for nearly 15 years. However, standouts were few and far between, and largely relegated to the paranormal genre. US offerings were also propped up by outside contributions (e.g., the brilliant *Let the Right One In* [2008]).[2] Yet overall, the broad picture of horror film in the US was a creatively stagnant one, with even noteworthy contributions hamstrung by the overwhelming familiarity of the plot. Between 2000 and 2013, 24 movies made the Rotten Tomatoes Top 100 rated horror films.[3] However, since 2014, a whopping 20 films have made the list.[4] Recency bias aside, a glance at the list of recent additions shows a distinct tonal shift, with innovative characters and ideas crossing a wide swath of different subgenres. Amidst a wave of excellent horror films, *It Follows* was one of the first, and it helped redefine the genre.

On the face of it, the plot of *It Follows* could be a metaphor for sexually-transmitted diseases or a cautionary tale about teenage intercourse. Yet, the film's director, who generally insists on individuals interpreting his film however they see fit, dismisses this interpretation:

> I certainly was aware of the connection with STDs and many of these other sorts of subtexts to the film, and I kind of tried to sprinkle a few different clues around. I think it's very easy to see it in different ways. You can see some of these things in a very literal way, and I also think that you can step back and view them as something larger as opposed to it just being about sex and STDs. (Crump 2015)

Mitchell pulls his inspiration for *It Follows* from a variety of sources, leaning heavily on John Carpenter, as so many horror directors do, but also including *Creature from the Black Lagoon* (1954) for the dogged nature of the entity, *Cat People* (1942) for the climactic pool scene, and *Paris, Texas* (1984) for so many of the suburban details. Plenty about the film is great: acting, writing, plot, pacing, characters, dialogue. Helmed by a director who long had an interest in horror but for whom this was his first foray into the genre, it's beautifully, eerily shot with a distinct, unsettling atmosphere. But the true brilliance of *It Follows* is its self-awareness within the genre, borrowing and building off a plethora of elements from other subgenres with a confidence normally reserved for satire. But here, no one's laughing. This straight-laced, sentient film occupies the space between sex and death, openly embracing what so many horror films—particularly slasher movies—could not acknowledge, which is one of the many reasons it has garnered so much attention and praise.

Before I begin heaping even more attention and praise on *It Follows*, a couple of quick clarifications. The entity in the film that changes forms has been referred to in many different ways: the follower, the force, the being (on-set, Mitchell would refer to it as an 'it', preceded by a descriptor: 'the giant it'). I'll be referring to 'it' as the 'entity', while specifying what form the entity was taking at the time of the observation being discussed, though I'll use 'it' as a pronoun to avoid 'entity' overload. Plenty of other horror films will be discussed, some in passing, others at length. I will attempt to refer to the characters in these films in ways that will be most identifiable; in some instances that might be the name of the actor or actress, in others it might be the name of the character. Social media observations, online forum analysis, and critics eager to deconstruct a brilliant piece of art are (wonderfully) all-too-prevalent online, and I'll reference such discussions and source material whenever relevant. I'll occasionally refer to an earlier version of the script to better understand what decisions shaped the final product. While a group of such critics appear on the DVD disc commentary, no director's track exists. However, Mitchell conducted several different interviews and provided nuanced, thoughtful responses, all of which helped with the analysis. Hopefully you agree.

FOOTNOTES

1. The former RADiUS-TWC CEO Tom Quinn said the release window was going to be changed, 'unbeknownst to the VOD providers', explaining, 'We had to straight-up lie to VOD providers. That was a placeholder date'. Fortunately for all involved, 'Almost all of the COD providers were super cool about it' (Buder 2015).

2. Horror was also immeasurably assisted by the rebirth of the uniquely-positioned (and exceedingly tricky) hybrid comedy-horror subgenre (*Cabin in the Woods* [2012], *Severance* [2006], *Behind the Mask: The Rise of Leslie Vernon* [2007], and *Tucker and Dale vs. Evil* [2010]), with the films 'adhering to the conventions of the slasher film and disrupting the narrative... with metacommentary on the genre' (Jackson, 2016).

3. This is an admittedly flawed methodology, though it's a far more accurate predictor of quality than the box office, which lists the top-grossing horror movies from 2010-2012 as *Paranormal Activity 2* (2010), *Paranormal Activity 3* (2011), and *Paranormal Activity 4* (2012).

4. *Get Out* (2017), *The Babadook* (2014), *It Follows* (2015), *The Witch* (2016), *Under the Shadow* (2016), *The Love Witch* (2016), *A Girl Walks Home Alone at Night* (2014), *Green Room* (2016), *Train to Busan* (2016), *We Are Still Here* (2015), *Raw* (2017), *Don't Breathe* (2016), *Bone Tomahawk* (2015), *Spring* (2015), *Goodnight Mommy* (2015), *The Autopsy of Jane Doe* (2017), *It Comes at Night* (2017), *Backcountry* (2015), *A Field in England* (2014), *The Conjuring 2* (2016).

CHAPTER 1: 'A HINT OF JOY BEFORE IT ALL GOES TO HELL'

It Follows opens on a tree-lined suburban street outside Detroit at dusk. Mitchell has repeatedly listed John Carpenter as one of his main influences (Fear 2015), and this is apparent here—it might as well be *Halloween*'s (1978) Haddonfield's sister city. Everything's quiet, apart from errant birds chirping, and the camera pans to reveal a two-story brick house. A young woman bursts out of the front door, sprinting awkwardly in red stilettos across the front lawn and into the street. Along with pumps, she's wearing a translucent, unsupportive side-cut top with comfortable short-shorts, suggesting that she was likely heading to bed, despite what her footwear suggests.[1] She stops in the street and locks eyes on something out of frame and doesn't stop staring, even when a neighbour asks if she needs help. Off camera, her father calls her by name and asks if she is okay. Annie, breathing heavily, insists she's fine.[2] She takes off running again, circling deliberately around an invisible obstacle, passing her father to run indoors before bolting back outside, climbing into a car, and driving away. The next time we see Annie, she's sitting on the edge of a lake, lit by the warm glow of her car's headlights, water lapping behind her as she leaves a farewell voicemail for her parents. The next morning, she's dead, her brutalised corpse sprawled out on the beach.

The horror prologue is an essential component to the genre, typically serving as a 'portent of things to come (like a mini trailer), a justification of the monster or as a way of keeping the audience tense, aware that they are watching a horror film and not a drama' (Odell & Le Blanc, 2010: 14). Here, the opening vignette is striking, more so than a typical horror film opening that features the killer attacking. For starters, there's no evidence of the murderer: no mask, no weapon. We don't see the killer, and though that's somewhat expected—saving the reveal is fairly common for horror films—here the threat never materialises; the prologue starts out with a long, continuous wide shot rather than convoluted close-ups to hide the killer's form. However, while the audience learns very little about the killer, we can glean one important detail: its apparently limitless range. So many prologues ground the threat in a specific location, be it a haunted house, a campground, or a town. Here we see the victim flee not only on foot, but by vehicle, from the streets of suburbia to the middle of nowhere. Yet it's to no avail.

And throughout the chase, there's no indication that the threat exists anywhere but in Annie's mind. The hints of concern are overridden by the tone of confusion, with the audience uncertain of Annie's frantic focus. Until the shot of her bloodied body at the water's edge, the audience is watching one side of a horror film where the danger might not even be real.

We're then introduced to Jay Height (Maika Monroe), floating in her above-ground pool, amused by two neighbourhood boys conspicuously ogling her. She goes inside to get ready for a date, stopping in the living room to chat with her younger sister, Kelly, and their friends, Yara and Paul. Mitchell deliberately avoids dating the piece by having technology from a variety of eras—here they're all watching *Killers from Space* (1954) on an analogue television while Yara sits on the couch, reading a compact that seems to have a Kindle screen and bars denoting a wireless data signal; unofficially dubbed the 'shell phone' by Mitchell, this product is actually just an e-reader in a '60s shell compact designed for the film and does not currently exist.[3] The purpose here is not only to avoid dating the film—similar to how classics like *Halloween* avoid attempts at teenage slang—but also to create a world where the audience connects to the overall experience rather than specific moments. As Mitchell explains, 'It's not so much about a teenager in the moment, in this exact day or year. It's kind of more of a reflection, or a memory, mixed with something made up' (Crump, 2015).

It Follows was Mitchell's second film—his first, *The Myth of the American Sleepover* (2011), followed a group of teens on a single Friday night in Detroit. It's marvellously subdued and thoughtful, and despite a slew of locations and the usual hormones, it's marked by its lack of drama; critic Grady Smith wrote that it 'feels like a John Hughes script directed by Gus Van Sant' (Smith, 2011). *Sleepover* played a role in creating the world of *It Follows*, with Mitchell explaining:

> I sort of thought that it would be fun to start from sort of a basepoint from a similar world, to imagine characters that could have existed within that first film, and I aged them up a little bit and imagined how they might react or deal with being placed in a nightmare. (Crump, 2015)

His ability to capture the natural cadence of teen interaction grounds the film, contrasted with so many others in the genre that rely on an expository blast of bawdy dialogue and topical references. In this first visit with the protagonists, we immediately understand the group's dynamics: Jay is older than Kelly but they're still close, Yara is an outlier, and Paul is hopelessly in love with Jay. When Jay walks away to prepare for her date with Hugh, Paul stares longingly at her departure while Yara shakes her head in disapproval at the transparency of his affection. All of this is established in just over a minute of screen time, and it's this effortless depiction of teenage relationships that not only grounds the film with emotional weight, but also allows the focus to be on the impending danger of the entity.

While on their date, Jay and Hugh are seated in a movie theatre, waiting for the feature to start, still playing a game where they try to guess who the other would trade lives with. We know nothing about Hugh, something that doesn't really change as the movie progresses. Suddenly, a clearly distressed Hugh abruptly asks Jay to leave the building; outdoors, while Jay peppers him with questions about who he saw, Hugh simply says he felt sick. Despite the bizarre behaviour, he recovers to salvage the evening, as Jay chalks the whole thing up to him seeing an ex-girlfriend in the theatre. It's not their last date, but we're unsure how many more there are because of Mitchell's use of contrasting indicators regarding the passage of time. The next day, Jay and Kelly are walking home together, surrounded by lush greenery, Kelly in jean shorts and a cardigan while Jay wears boots and a winter coat. They glance across the street a few times, and once the camera cuts to a group of kids playing football in the front yard with a light dusting of fallen maple leaves on the ground and hints of brown and yellow in the tree. These are the only leaves on the ground we see their entire trek home. Yet days later, through the window of Jay's classroom, we see the mostly-bare remnants of late autumn's abscission. Mitchell's technique is effective at creating unease in the film, but it also works to shore up any minor plotlines; any questions about how Jay talked to Hugh about the disturbance, whether she waited awhile before deciding to forgive his behaviour, or any other meaningless minutia are avoided, streamlining the film while simultaneously shoring up the characters.

Regardless of when Jay and Hugh meet up again, on their next date the two spend a relaxing evening making out on a deserted beach before having sex in the back of his car.[4] Jay's not a virgin, and it's not a traumatic experience. As Mitchell said, 'When Jay sleeps with Hugh, I think there's still a melancholy there, but I do think there's some hint of joy before it all goes to hell—at least from Jay's point of view' (Nastasi, 2015). But afterwards, Hugh chloroforms Jay, and she wakes up in an abandoned building, strapped to a wheelchair while Hugh stares into the distance. He assures her that he isn't going to hurt her, that this is the only way to get her to listen to his warning because something is coming for her. The thing or 'it', as he describes, which was passed to him and now he has passed to Jay, can look like anyone, but there's only one of it. This entity soon emerges from the darkness in the form of a naked middle-aged woman, walking slowly, deliberately, directly toward Jay. Hugh continues with the exposition: It's very slow but it's not dumb, so never go into a place that only has one exit. If it kills her, it will come after him, 'so don't let it touch you'. Jay screams for help, and before the woman can reach her, Hugh wheels Jay out of danger. In the next scene, he pulls up in front of Jay's house where Kelly, Yara and Paul are playing cards on the patio. Car running, Hugh pulls Jay out of the backseat and sets her on the ground, saying 'Don't let it touch you' before leaving. Clad only in her pink bra and underwear, her hands bound together, Jay staggers forward and collapses in her yard as the trio sprints over to see if she's okay. Jay is interviewed by police and placed in the hospital for observation, but it's immediately clear that the authorities are having no success. After shots of Jay struggling with what has happened to her, we see her sitting in a classroom at Wayne State University. This is the first time Jay will meet an entity on her own.

The scene evokes a similar staging in *Halloween*. The first time Laurie Strode sees Michael Myers, she is sitting in her high school classroom, pen against her mouth between taking diligent notes as she glances out of the nearby window. Carpenter cuts to a point-of-view shot to capture a glimpse of Michael Myers staring at her from behind the stolen station wagon. Laurie looks down momentarily, but when she looks back up he's still there, unmoving, still watching. Their visual exchange is only interrupted by the teacher's question (about fate and destiny, no less), which a visibly shaken Laurie answers perfectly. Jay also first notices her adversary while sitting in the classroom, but the differences between the scenes are stark. In *Halloween*, the camera starts out at the front of the classroom, and slowly pulls in on Laurie. In *It Follows*, the audience is thrown into the middle of an unfamiliar classroom with no sign of our heroine; the especially observant might notice Greg's profile toward the front of the class, but otherwise, there's no real anchor until the camera pans around the room and lands on

Jay, who (like Laurie) is sitting in the back of the classroom. This English class is a lecture rather than a discussion, so Jay is not granted the same opportunity to demonstrate her literary acumen to the audience. After Jay sees the entity approach, she exits the classroom as the professor calls out 'Excuse me!', apparently unaware of Jay's name despite the small class size. But crucially, the scene begins with an innovative motif Mitchell continues throughout the film: the 360-degree pan.

Throughout the film, Mitchell said they tried to keep the camera close to the actors' location, 'so if there's a point-of-view shot from their perspective, we didn't necessarily throw a longer lens on so that that form of the monster would be closer and clearer.' When storyboarding the film, Mitchell said he and his cinematographer (Mike Gioulakis) 'wanted to really sort of put the audience into the scenes in the sense that you feel like you're actually in that environment with them so it's very experiential in a way. You can look into the distance, look under the edges of the frame' (Nemiroff, 2015). The use of the 360° pan accomplishes just this. Its deployment in *It Follows* is both frequent and effective, providing the audience a unique glimpse into the experiences of the potential victims.

After all, the killer's POV shot is a slasher staple, famously remembered in Detective Arbogast's trip backward down the stairs in *Psycho* (1960) or in the sojourn by six-year-old Michael Myers around the house and up the stairs. The 360° pan is a rarity, particularly in horror. For filmmakers to cede control for leading the audience through a scene is understandably difficult, as horror staples such as jump scares, cat scares and mirror scares rely on directional camerawork; a simple wide shot at the wrong moment ruins the setup, allowing a chance for audiences to peer around the room to avoid such surprises. In horror, the need to lead is amplified for precisely that reason: the fright typically comes from the startle, not the setup. This technique mirrors the effect achieved when using security footage, which Julia Leyda argues ironically creates more anxiety for the viewers in films like the *Paranormal Activity* series. 'Positioning the camera in a non-human POV, the movie produces an uncanny sense of helplessness; we occupy neither the demon's perspective nor the sleeping characters', but that of a machine, the diegetic digital camera' (2014: 420). The use of this 360° pan, while rare, is surprisingly effective, allowing audiences to experience this dread of recognition that the heroine feels; when the audience catches a glimpse of the approaching disguised murderer, it triggers a pang of Leyda's helplessness as we cannot intervene. In doing so, this strengthens the parasocial relationship we have with the heroine, as the audience identifies with the struggle to identify the threat. Incidentally, this is paired with a twinge of guilt at a split-second feeling of success for finding the hidden killer like some morbid version of *Where's Waldo?* (or *Wally*, in the UK). Beneath this emotional resonance, however, is simple unease; because this technique is so rarely used in a horror film, the drastic style shift adds to the unsettled ambiance Mitchell has painstakingly constructed.

Once Jay looks out the classroom window, her expression quickly morphs from one of confusion into fear. There is something different—not wholly unnatural, just different—about the old woman walking slowly toward her. We first notice the woman standing directly in front of the wall of a building with no visible door or open window; not enough to trigger a mental alarm, but enough for the eye to be drawn to that form slowly making its way across the quad. No one else on the ground seems to be paying her any attention, even though it's the only thing we the audience can see. She's old… like, really old. There's no law against an elderly person visiting the campus of a public university, but it underscores the surrealism of the disparate figure inching closer to the screen. Even from a distance, the bright white outfit stands in stark contrast to the overcast, autumnal dreariness, and the closer she gets, the audience sees that she's wearing a white nightgown, her pale, exposed arms and legs further contrasted against the hoodies and heavy jackets worn by the students. The situation's oddness turns to fear and is ultimately too much. After Jay flees the classroom (as classmate Greg looks on in a mixture of curiosity and concern), she walks nervously through the hall, glancing over her shoulder as the old woman rounds the corner. We see her clearly now, the camera alternating from long shot to medium shot. The woman is emotionless, her face a blank slate, and her pace doesn't waver, even as Jay fully recognises the threat. Jay turns and runs out of the door, rushing to her car and driving warily out of danger.

Jay meets with Kelly and Paul at the ice cream shop where they work. Jay explains what happened and Paul suggests staying the night to make sure she's safe. Jay and Kelly simultaneously reject the offer, but once he clarifies he would stay on the couch to protect her, Jay relents. Later that night, Jay comes downstairs to hang out with Paul because she cannot sleep, and the two talk fondly of their memories together. The sexual tension is palpable and building to something when they both hear glass shatter from the kitchen. Paul goes to investigate and finds nothing, but Jay goes to double-check just to be sure. Slowly winding her way down the hallway (a short walk but Mitchell uses seven shots to get there), Jay slowly turns toward the audience; the only time in the entire film where a character is shown in slow motion or looking directly into the camera. Standing in the middle of the tile floor is a young woman with a bloodied face and torn clothing, walking slowly forward while urinating down her leg. Horrified, Jay stumbles up the stairs and locks herself in her room. Kelly and Paul come into her room to console her, but when they open the door for Yara, a tall man emerges from the darkness, peering through the door as he moves closer, targeting Jay. She screams and climbs out of the window to escape; the audience sees the tall man in pursuit, but Kelly, Paul and Yara are left in the dark, vacillating between concern and confusion while Jay disappears into the night.

This is the second time Jay is ousted from her everyday life by the entity, which is somewhat unique in the horror genre. A film featuring a young woman hanging out with her friends while being stalked by a seemingly unstoppable killer is typically located in a non-urban location isolated from civilisation where unsuspecting teens won't be missed. James Kendrick points out that these settings are typically connected directly with the experience of American adolescents, such as summer camps, high schools, colleges and small-town suburbia. *It Follows* overachieves and manages to hit several places, with stops at college, home, a vacation home and a swimming pool. It's not uncommon for a horror movie to set up shop in a single location where the conflict will ultimately take place. In *Men, Women and Chainsaws* (1992), her seminal book on gender in the horror genre, Carol Clover notes that a key trope in the slasher film is the so-called 'Terrible Place', a location where all victims eventually end up and have to fight for their lives. In *It Follows*, Jay soon finds the Terrible Place to be *wherever she is*. This approach actually heightens suspense rather than disorientating the viewer, as it underscores the serious, all-encompassing nature of the threat. Regardless of her location, Jay cannot find sanctuary. One by one, she abandons her places of comfort because they are invaded by this menacing, determined force. By travelling to other locations, by seeking refuge in a variety of places that a young adult might find solace, Jay actually shrinks her own universe; this tactic has a counterintuitive effect, revealing how vulnerable she is to this particular threat.

Following her in-home close encounters with the two forms of the entity, Jay flees on a borrowed bike to a nearby park where she waits on a swing set, eyes focused on the sparsely lit horizon for either friend or foe. A trio of the former arrives first, as Kelly greets her sobbing sister with a long hug and reassurances. They're followed shortly by Greg, a young man who lives across the street and to this point has been dancing around the periphery of these main characters; he was sitting with a date in his car when he saw Jay burst from her home and pedal down the street, all through his rearview mirror. Paul explains that someone broke into the house, and Jay announces she doesn't want to go home, she wants to go and find Hugh. Greg volunteers his car, and by the time Detroit starts to wake up, they're all en route to Hugh's house.[5] When they arrive at the now-deserted, decaying home, they're treated to a glimpse of his bizarre (but justifiably so), paranoid life. Windows are covered with old newspapers and rigged with aluminum cans as a crude warning system. Homemade escape hatches to other rooms prevent anyone from being trapped. In a stack of pornographic magazines next to a bare mattress, Paul finds an old photo of Hugh wearing a letterman jacket. They recognise the high school and go visit, asking someone in the front office to see an old yearbook. There they learn that Hugh's real name is Jeff, and they head to his real home to confront him about what's happening.[6] Hugh's mother answers the door, and Jay is momentarily taken aback as she recognises his mom as the same nude woman in the abandoned building that had walked toward Jay while she screamed helplessly from a wheelchair. Hugh's mother invites them all in, and soon the group is sitting with Hugh in his backyard. There he expounds on the brief warning he had given Jay in the abandoned building. Hugh mentioned that he had a one-night stand with someone he didn't know, saying 'I think that's where it came from'. This is a complicated statement because Hugh is either saying that he thinks that's where he caught it or that he thinks that's where it originated. Regardless, he continues talking, explaining that he can still see the entity and is still very much in danger, and the entity will continue to pursue Jay until she passes it along to someone else. He reminds Jay that the entity can only walk, and so she might want to drive somewhere and consider infecting someone else. With Jay still refusing to go back home, Greg drives her, Paul, Kelly and Yara to his family's lake house.

The drive around Detroit and into the country allows Mitchell to showcase his film's music, a tour de force of synthesisers and driving beats. Critic Matt Barone argues that recent horror movie scores generally take one of three forms: Carpenter knock-offs, 'non-descript orchestral arrangements' in the tradition of John Williams and Bernard Herrmann, or soft, vague tones with the occasional loud burst of noise intended to startle the audience (2015). *It Follows*' score is another welcome departure from horror movie trends, with a rich electronic sound that is at once catchy but not overpowering, otherworldly but grounded in the genre's reality, and refreshingly unique to pair with the innovative story unfolding onscreen. Mitchell explained he wanted something that would stand out:

> …something really bold and memorable. Something that was beautiful, but could also genuinely affect people and create anxiety. The goal was to fluctuate between beautiful melodies and controlled noise — the kind of thing that nearly assaults the audience with the sound. (Nastasi, 2015)

For the soundtrack, Mitchell recruited Disasterpeace, the stage name for musician Rich Vreeland, who specialies in electronic music. Originally Vreeland was told he'd have six months to compose, but that deadline was reduced to just three weeks once *It Follows* was accepted to Cannes. That synth-heavy temporary score set the foundation for what became an unnerving, otherworldly soundtrack that is truly unique. Vreeland said he really is not a big horror fan and didn't know much about Carpenter's work, but believes 'synths can create sounds that are not always analogous to real life sounds. I think that tendency can ignite the imagination. It's perfect fodder for writing scary music' (Anderson, 2016).

The lake house offers a brief respite from urban landscape, with stately maples lining the long driveway, an expansive lawn hemmed in by thick woods, and a calm, grey-blue lake hovering in the background. Greg soon trudges out to the boathouse and removes a handgun from an old tackle box, setting up cereal boxes for Jay to use as target practice. The two sort-of reminisce, with the laconic Greg reminding a taciturn Jay that he's across the street if she ever needs him. She responds, 'I remember', a reminder that the two used to be involved. The next scene features Jay, Greg, Kelly and Paul sitting out on the beach, the sand still clinging to moisture from a recent storm. It's a surprisingly sombre event given the setting, the intermittent sunshine forcing a combination of long sleeves and shorts (except for Kelly, who dons a bikini top and short-shorts). The group sits in silence drinking beer, stealing glances at one another before gazing back down to resume drinking and fidgeting. Behind Jay, off in the distance, we see Yara slowly walking to join the group. Kelly and Greg share a sexual, awkward moment of eye contact before he leaves to urinate in the nearby bushes, wordlessly passing by the approaching Yara on his way. In a delightful twist, the camera focuses on Paul with the lake in the background, which is when we see Yara goofily paddle into the frame on a pink inner tube, revealing that the person we thought was Yara heading toward the group is actually the entity taking Yara's form, moving steadily, relentlessly forward.

As the sisters decide to get into the water, Kelly's face turns from excited optimism to a look of stunned horror as Jay's long, blonde hair mysteriously is held aloft by the invisible entity. Jay screams as it pulls her hair, the rest of the group concerned but confused as she's locked in battle with an unseen force. Paul swings wildly with a lawn chair and hits the entity, jarring Jay loose, though Paul is in turn struck violently and flies off-screen. Jay, Yara and Kelly sprint toward the boat house with Paul running past entity-Yara in pursuit, all while Greg returns from his call of nature just in time to see the group scatter. Inside the boathouse, Jay grabs the handgun from the tackle box and begins firing at the entity while Greg dives for cover behind a flimsy lawn chair, confused and panicked as his crush blasts away at a threat only she can see. Amidst the gunfire, a shot hits the entity in the neck, blood splattering into the air as entity-Yara collapses on the ground… momentarily. Jay slams the door closed just as it begins to stand up again. After the entity (this time a young boy) kicks a hole in the door and begins to climb through, Jay escapes through the other door and sprints toward the car. The entity again shifts forms to a different young woman before resuming its form as Yara. Jay hops into the driver's seat, her friends calling her name as she drives away.

Jay's joyride does not last long. A few miles down the road she swerves to miss a truck and crashes into a cornfield. She wakes up in a hospital bed, a gash on her forehead and her broken wrist in a cast. Lying in bed, she stares at the door, transfixed by the mundane noise of a nurse walking down the hallway. She tears her gaze away from the door to lock eyes with Greg, the unspoken message clear. That evening, we see the two having sex in her hospital bed, Greg absorbed in the moment of ecstasy, Jay staring listlessly at the door. The next day at the hospital, the two hold hands in her room while Paul seethes outside. Jay nervously asks if Greg has seen the entity, and Greg assures her he has not. Later, when everyone's back at home, Greg stops by to talk to Jay only to be stonewalled by her friends, explaining she was holed up in her room and in no condition to talk to anyone. They also ask if he's seen anything suspicious, and he confesses as he walks away that he doesn't believe the entity actually exists. As far as horror movie tropes go, he might as well have said, 'I'll be right back'.

That night, Jay sleeplessly stares out of the window at the lit suburban street when she notices someone out for a walk. It's Greg, but he's barefoot and wearing long underwear with a white shirt. Realisation hits Jay that this is the entity, which is confirmed seconds later when entity-Greg breaks a window and climbs through. Reminiscent of a scene from *A Nightmare on Elm Street* (1984), Jay frantically calls Greg's house to warn him, but no one answers. She races across the street and climbs through the broken window, screaming for Greg as she races to the top of the stairs. There, she sees Greg's mother pounding incessantly on the door. Greg opens to see his mom standing there, her open robe revealing her bare left breast. Wordlessly, she leaps on him like a wild animal, driving him back onto the floor of his room. Startled, Jay instinctively steps backward as if to leave, but then walks warily to his door instead, peering inside Greg's room. There she sees Mrs. Hannigan straddling her son's lifeless body, grinding against him while interlocking her fingers with his, the whole scene gruesomely lit by a fallen, flickering lamp. Jay staggers backward and runs out of the house, hopping in her car and driving away as entity-Greg emerges from the house, walking determinedly toward his next target.

Greg's demise is viscerally disturbing, more so than the gore audiences typically see in the violent death of a discarded sex partner in a horror film. Movie killers (particularly those in slasher films) typically use some type of stabbing implement, such as a machete, knife, pickaxe, or even a corkscrew. A gun is far more effective but also a rarity, and with good reason. James Kendrick notes that 'not only do stabbings, garrotings, and gougings allow for the ample deployment of gory make-up effects…they also emphasize the close proximity of the killer and victim'. Rather than being killed from a distance with a gun, the up-close act of stabbing is 'a deeply personal, physically close violent action that leaves a lingering sense of discomfort in the viewer' (Kendrick, 2017: 319). Here Mitchell makes the murder even more intimate, which makes the act that much more disturbing. Parents can be killers—just ask Jason Voorhees' mom—but rarely are they killing their offspring. If we see a murderous mother or father, it's likely because she or he is possessed, a la *The Conjuring* (2013) or *The Amityville Horror* (1979). Again, Mitchell exhibits an impressive understanding of what makes an aspect of the horror film frightening without simply duplicating what's come before; it's the difference between innovative filmmaking and slasher simulacrum.

Jay drives into the countryside before stopping in the middle of the woods, seemingly at random. She climbs out of the car and lays on the hood, looking up into the night sky before falling asleep outdoors, likely so she doesn't get trapped in the car by the entity should it approach before she awakens. Given the genre's penchant for terrorising teens in a rural setting, Jay's apparent preference for the dark, unknown wilderness as opposed to the familiar confines of the city makes for an intriguing contrast. When she wakes up in the great outdoors, amidst the chirping of birds Jay hears music in the distance. Walking through the woods and then reeds, she reaches the shoreline and sees the source of the generic rock: a speedboat anchored just offshore, with three young men inside. Pausing momentarily, she walks gingerly along the rocky beach to the edge of the water before stripping down to her pink underwear and tank top. She begins to wade into the water before a smash cut to Jay driving home, her cast soaked, her hair still wet. She pulls in to the driveway where Kelly and Yara are dutifully sitting on the porch, waiting.

Mitchell's intentionally vague sense of time on-screen adds to the confusion following the scene at the edge of the lake. Following Jay's arrival home, we see a shot of the Height family pool, empty, with one side collapsed. At first, the audience likely assumes a struggle, but an interior shot of the above-ground pool shows the damage is intentional, with one portion removed and the pool drained to be cleaned. This is likely to show the passage of time. Yet we soon see Jay asleep in her room, wearing the same outfit she had on at the lake. This is further complicated by the (seemingly random) shot of a plate of food. This shot was mirrored earlier, after Jay returned home from the hospital following the night with Hugh in the abandoned building. The camera focuses on a tray holding a glass of orange juice and a plate that has a bologna sandwich, Doritos and a pickle spear on it, as well as a blue napkin with a round, white pill.

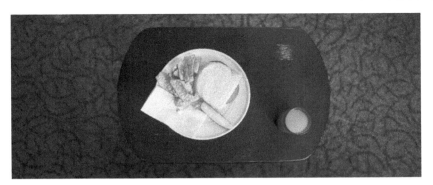

Healthy plate...

Fifty minutes of the movie after this, Jay has returned from the lake and is asleep on the floor (with Kelly and Yara on the bed), and the camera lingers on the same glass of orange juice next to the same plate—the pill is gone, but the number of Doritos remains the same (there are 11). However, in this shot, the pickle is shriveled, the meat is darkened, and there is visible mold growing in the middle of the sandwich.

...moldy plate.

I again call attention to this device not simply because it's incredibly effective (and surprisingly underutilised by its horror brethren, though that will likely change following the success of *It Follows*), but also to demonstrate how strategically it's used. It's never a technique to bail its heroes out of a seemingly un-escapable situation *deus ex machina* style, nor is it used to highlight a contrast so severe that it disrupts the flow of the film.

This strategy also works at a number of levels, but perhaps the most effective aspect is that the audience is unaware of how long the entity has actually been after Jay. Not knowing *when* exactly the entity began its pursuit also casts doubt on *where* exactly the entity is at any given time. As Hugh warned, no matter where it is, it's walking toward Jay, but by disrupting the film's timeline, the audience is constantly uncertain as to how close it might be. Any shot at doing SAT-style math ('Jay drives 74 miles away, and the entity walks at 3 mph. How long…') is undone, and like Jay we're forced to rely on scanning the horizon while questioning everyone's identity.

With Jay, Kelly, and Yara spread out across the entire room, Paul enters and talks to her about Greg's death, learning that she 'chose' Greg because she thought he could protect himself, which seems to place Paul at ease; at least it wasn't true love, so a glimmer of hope remains. He tentatively holds her hand and leans in for a kiss, but Jay—wary of his intentions—turns her head away and goes to look out of the window. He notices a photo of Jay swimming, inspiration strikes, and Paul hints that he has an idea for defeating the entity once and for all. The group loads up the car and drives away, but not before Jay looks up and sees the entity standing astride the apex of the roof. They drive through some dilapidated neighbourhoods before parking the car south of 8 Mile around dusk, walking the rest of the way while lugging suitcases and reminiscing about how their parents used to warn them about this part of the city. They arrive at a chain link fence, beyond which sits a natatorium, towering above an empty field like some ancient mausoleum. They break in and immediately start pulling out small appliances from their bags—electronic typewriter, TV, lamp, space heater—and line them up along the edge of the pool. It's quickly apparent that Paul's plan is to lure the entity into the water in an attempt to electrocute it, and on its face, the plan seems fundamentally flawed.[7] Once the devices are plugged in, Jay climbs slowly into the pool and wades into the middle, each of her friends scanning the room for any sign of the intruder. As a violent thunderstorm rages outside, Jay remains in the water, but the wait tries everyone else's vigilance, with Yara's attention wandering back to her shell phone, Kelly lazily dangling her arm in the pool, and Paul restlessly alternating between checking the doors and staring off into space. It's actually one of several small but significant moments where Mitchell slows the film down. This not only lets the film breathe—creating a natural contrast that allows suspense to rise and fall—but it also allows for the characters to be themselves, to be (at times) attention-addled young adults who clearly care for their friend's plight but also have never seen the threat themselves, which makes for a monotonous stakeout.

Soon the audience catches a glimpse of the killer's POV—the only such instance in the entire film—as it walks down a long, narrow hallway filled with the sound of filters and pumps. In the next shot, Jay turns to look at the door and gasps, saying it just walked into the room. Kelly asks what she sees, and Jay confesses that she doesn't want to tell her. Paul tells her to point at it, and Jay does just that, tracking something the audience cannot see as it circles the water while the camera slowly pans along with her unspoken directions. Suddenly one of the devices levitates and rockets toward Jay, splashing next to her in the water as she lunges out of the way. The lights in the pool flicker, going dark momentarily as the electric current ineffectually fizzles out. Paul shouts that it didn't work, with Yara sighing in relief—Jay remains un-electrocuted—but the reprieve is brief as the entity, now visible to the audience as a middle-aged man in a white tank top and white boxers, continues to hurl appliances at his target with startling accuracy. The plan in shambles, Paul fumbles in his bag for Plan B—Greg's handgun from the lake house.

Paul fires from a distance, but because he cannot see the entity, he shoots Yara in the calf by accident. Kelly rushes to help her while Paul continues to shuffle cautiously toward Jay—oblivious to the harm he has caused—asking her to keep pointing at the entity. Paul continues to fire somewhat blindly, while the entity relentlessly heaves items at Jay. At one point, Paul gets close, and when the entity holds up its hand, Paul shoots a bullet through the entity's palm, splattering blood all over the wall.[8] Meanwhile, Kelly roots through a bag, grabs a bed sheet, and starts fanning it through the air. It lands and Paul finally has a target: a human form draped in a blanket. He shoots the entity in the head, and it falls (bed sheet and all) into the water. Jay rushes toward the pool's edge but is immediately pulled down by the entity and held under. Paul empties his gun into the water, striking the entity on the top of its head. Kelly and Paul help pull Jay out of the water. As she tries to catch her breath and clutches her red, swollen ankle where the entity held her in its grasp, Paul asks if it's still there, if she can see it. Paul looks into the pool, and we see only clear-blue chlorinated water. Jay inches toward the edge and peers into the pool, only to see a rapidly expanding, ominous cloud of blood spreading through the water.

In the next shot, Jay is straddling Paul on the couch in her living room with a chair barricading the door, both underneath a blanket as she wordlessly begins having sex with him, both breathing heavily with pleasure while rain pours outside the window. Post-coitus, the two ask one another if they feel any different (they don't). In the following scene, Jay stares sleeplessly off the edge of her bed while her mom rubs Jay's back; the camera focuses on an old family photo in the background, revealing that the form the entity took at the pool was that of her father, which would explain why she didn't want to tell Kelly what she was seeing. Meanwhile, we see Paul driving around abandoned buildings eyeing prostitutes, most likely to pass on the entity to someone that would (strategically) pass it along to another victim. In the final scene, the sun is setting as Paul and Jay walk hand-in-hand (technically hand-in-cast, suggesting little time has passed) down the sidewalk in their neighborhood. A middle-aged man rakes leaves as they walk by, and Jay taps Paul's fingers with her own. This is likely a signal the two have worked out, a way of identifying a potential threat to be sure both have seen it. In this case, since the entity will come for Paul before killing Jay, she's undoubtedly making sure Paul's ready to run lest the guy doing yardwork is actually the entity in disguise. They continue to walk past the man, and before the credits roll, we see a figure walking down the sidewalk behind them.

FOOTNOTES

1. Mitchell himself acknowledges the confusing contrast, saying it was a deliberate choice as a play on the conventions of women in horror movies.
2. In a possible nod to Carpenter, her name (Annie) is also the first of Laurie Strode's friends to be murdered in John Carpenter's 1978 classic *Halloween* (though Annie was also the name of the first of the new camp counselors to be killed off in *Friday the 13th* [1980] so it might just be a bad idea to be named Annie in a horror movie).
3. Some have suggested that the film's opening scene takes place in the present-day United States, and everything we see during the rest of the movie takes place in the past. It's an intriguing theory, as we see much more modern technology in the beginning (Annie uses a cell phone and drives a Subaru WRX), but the existence of the shell phone debunks that idea. If the film is taking place in the past, Yara shouldn't have access to an e-reader/cell phone because that technology wouldn't exist yet.
4. We get another hint of foreboding here, as Hugh's Ford Galaxy does not have license plates.

5. Earlier in the film, when she was being interviewed by police, Jay acknowledged she knew where he lived, but hadn't been inside because he seemed embarrassed of his home.

6. Despite finding out his real name, I'll be continuing to use the name 'Hugh' throughout this analysis for the sake of clarity.

7. For one thing, an Olympic-sized swimming pool is different than a bathtub.

8. Paul never reacts to the blood, and in subsequent shots there is no blood on the wall, which likely means only Jay would be able to actually see the carnage.

Chapter 2: Can't Stop, Won't Stop: Deconstructing The Entity

A horror film is only as effective as its threat, and one of the clearest ways that *It Follows* stands out from its horror brethren is the ingenious design and use of the entity. Opting for a shape-shifting killing machine instead of the traditional masked murderer, Mitchell added another dimension of suspense to an already-horrifying concept, particularly because when filming the entity, Mitchell had a specific reason for each form that the entity took:

> There are other forms that tie into other characters, too. Some are very clear and people get it, and some are much harder to pick up on. There are a couple that I don't think I've ever had anyone even ask about, because we also tried to be true to distance. (Buchanan, 2015)

The entity appears in nine different scenes, taking on a total of twelve different forms: A nude, middle-aged woman with brown hair approaching a deserted building; an elderly woman in a nightgown on Jay's college campus; a young woman with a bloodied mouth and torn top; a man in a plain white t-shirt with who is so tall he has to duck under Jay's bedroom door frame;[1] a redhead wearing a backpack outside of a high school; a Yara duplicate; a young boy wearing old-fashioned bib overall shorts; a familiar brunette; a Greg duplicate speed-walking in long underwear; a duplicate of Greg's mom wearing a white nightgown; a nude elderly man standing on Jay's roof; a duplicate of Jay's (deceased) father in a white tank top.[2]

Your standard slasher/stalker/serial killer is grounded by the fact that it's a human committing the murders, and so the individual cannot suddenly take flight or turn invisible. However, when introducing a new element to a film, the threat is only as effective as the rules surrounding it. For the entity, the basic rules are simple: It will follow you, it can look like anyone, it's slow (but not dumb), and you can get rid of it by sleeping with someone else. Hugh's vagueness on details in the initial encounter actually enhances the audience experience, eschewing the traditional explanation by a doctor, scientist or creator for one frantically, succinctly conveyed while the main character listens in terror. During this encounter, Hugh does make one important clarification:

It can look like people you know... or it can be a stranger in a crowd... whatever helps it get close to you. Sometimes I think it looks like people you love just to hurt you... scare you... make fun of you.

The best part of this explanation is how incomplete it is. Hugh's description is accurate but shallow and as Mitchell explains, might not fully capture the director's entire vision:

We understand what this monster is through one of the characters and he gives these rules to another character, but those rules are just things that he has figured out based on his own experiences and what he's seen, and maybe what he's heard from someone else – but unlikely if you hear the way he received it, if that's true. And so, they're not so much *my* rules. They're this guy's rules and he's probably mostly right, but there's a question of how accurate even he is. (Nemiroff, 2015)

We glean other rules as we move through the film. Apparently only those who are infected (or at least recently were infected) can see the entity, it cannot pass through walls, and if the entity doesn't appear as someone that the afflicted knows, it will appear as the person that it's imitating looked when that individual died. This could be why we see so many of the entity's forms with dark circles around their eyes, as though they've been staying awake to evade death for weeks.

The entity's ability to alter its form is incredibly effective. Hiding the killer is a time-honoured horror tradition, be it the infamous Bruce from *Jaws* (1975) or the more traditional Mrs. Voorhees; if it's not hiding the killer, it's about masking the killer's identity, typically… well… behind a mask. Regardless, the risk is that the more the audience sees the killer, the less scary it's likely to be. Prolonged exposure reveals not-so-special effects, questionable makeup, or other deal-breaking details, which is why the simpler the presentation, the more convincing the design; hence the *Friday the 13th* jumpsuit and mask. But by changing its form, Mitchell prevents any particular form from becoming too familiar, too scrutinised, which would render the fright inert. But beyond the frequency and form of its appearance, to appreciate the brilliance of the entity, you have to look at the being as an amalgam of horror mainstays.

A discussion of the entity begins with what it is not. It's not a bug-eyed alien, nor does it appear to come from outer space. In fact, its origins are not disclosed, which seems surprising; even the original *Invasion of the Body Snatchers* (1956) has a line of dialogue clarifying that the pods came from seeds drifting through space that took root in a farmer's field—a pointedly external threat rather than some wild animal, mad scientist's experiment or genetic mishap. The entity did not come from beneath the sea, beyond space, a land that time forgot, or the black lagoon. The fact that it can alter its shape, often taking the form of someone the victim recognises, might suggest pod people, but its motivation is not one of conquest, merely indifferent assignment. Mitchell said he does not like to explore the origins of the entity, declining to even reference a 'patient zero', stating, 'the moment you [try to solve the origins] then it becomes about magic or something else as opposed to a nightmare' (Nemiroff, 2015). This retains the entity's mystery, offering one less piece of information, and therefore one less potential weakness.

The entity mysteriously, gloriously refuses to fit into a particular identity. On its face, the natural fit is the supernatural: a demon, witch, ghost or some other metaphysical force that haunts and ultimately murders an unsuspecting target. A potential relative to the entity in *It Follows* would be Sadako/Samara from Hideo Nakata's *Ringu* (1998) and Gore Verbinski's remake, *The Ring* (2002), respectively. The question of what exactly Sadako is remains an unsettled one, but the mindless adherence to her mission mirrors that of the entity:

> Neither fully organic nor material, Sadako remains but an aberration in electronic transmission, a matrix error, a flicker of light, pain and loneliness transformed into a video image flowing out of the screen in a flood of pixels and shaping itself into a solid body, as if taking substance from the terror she inspires. She remains emotionless though born in a surge of emotions; she remains indifferent, as if programmed to repeat the curse, cursed herself, just as she was when she was still alive. (Ancuta, 2015)

Sadako is clearly supernatural – she can appear from reflective surfaces to murder her victims, who are killed in the same manner in which she died. Her innate urge to carry out her mission mirrors the entity's own need to seek out those who have violated some unwritten, unspoken code of sexual conduct. Just as Samara must kill with water, the entity apparently kills by raping its victim, draining his/her life force in the process, murdering in the same manner in which it was summoned. The fact that it kills by sex rather than with a weapon firmly sets the entity in the realm of demons, ghosts and spirits. As previously discussed, ghosts in cinema 'either take on the appearance of the living, replicating their idealized selves or their human condition prior to death, or they retain the horrific wounds that caused their demise' (Bishop, 2010: 21). And finally, the entity's ability to shift form to people the victim might know naturally creates unease as Jay (and the audience) attempts to determine why the entity is suddenly recognisable. The fact that the entity appears in different forms, trading out bodies in a matter of seconds, shows that the entity must be supernatural.

But the entity does not carry with it the symptoms of a supernatural infestation, least of all a demonic possession similar to Samara. A demoniac must be able to 'speak in tongues, levitate, have unusual strength, and be able to decrease the temperature in the room where he or she was' (Forcen, 2017: 79). Furthermore, it does not attach itself to someone or inhabit a living soul like a demonic force; none of the embodied seem sentient, as all we see is a different variation of a slow, surprisingly effective assassin. Also, it's not attaching itself to any one individual; the entity attaches itself to an *act*, personified by the latest victim, and it can easily be passed off onto someone else. Throw in the fact that religion is absent from the film (thereby negating the most obvious solution for possession) and the supernatural explanation becomes that much less likely. The entity's morphing ability suggests it might be a ghost, but a closer look reveals only that its origins are truly supernatural. Everything the entity does is hamstrung—to some extent—by rules of reality. For instance, the entity is invisible to all but the person it is stalking and former potential victims (Hugh can still see it even after he's passed the danger along to Jay), with bystanders only able to see the destruction in its wake. However, it's only invisible, not mystical. It's still hit by a lawn chair, it's still shot in the neck, and it can still have a sheet thrown over its form. When Paul shoots the bedsheet-covered entity in the head, blood from the wound is splattered against the off-white canvas before the being collapses into the water with a splash. The sheet, the splash, the shot—all of these are indicators of a physical being masked from sight rather than a spirit vacillating between tangible and intangible planes of existence.

At times, we'll see an entity begin to walk standing inches in front of a wall, implying that it ghosted through the side of a building, although we never witness such an act.

To the contrary, several times in the film we see the entity stymied by physical barriers, none of which are fortresses or bunkers. It throws rocks through windows to climb into homes and it even knocks on doors rather than kicking them down. In the boathouse, after Jay slams the door shut, we catch a glimpse of the entity having taken the form of the giant man we saw in Jay's room, setting up an assumption that he might kick in the door. Yet it only kicks a hole in the bottom of the door, small enough for its next form (the boy with the scarred face) to crawl through. A being that could materialise through walls would likely take a more direct approach. The only seemingly supernatural behaviour in terms of physical movement on the part of the entity is when the group leaves the house to execute Paul's pool plan. As they pull out of the driveway, Jay looks up and sees a naked man standing atop the roof, straddling the ridge line, glaring back at her. This is surprisingly unsettling, particularly since Jay does not warn her friends of his presence, the ingrained fear already normalised. However, the location of the entity is not necessarily otherworldly. Following Hugh's assault on Jay, she stands in her bra and underwear in her bathroom, staring at the mirror (and down her underwear) in trauma. The camera pulls back outside the bathroom to reveal a young boy hiding on the roof beneath her window. If an 8-year-old can climb up there, surely a non-supernatural entity can manage it.

The supernatural likely plays an important role in where it came from, how it kills, and how it's effective at remaining unseen. But beyond its unspoken origins and the invisibility, the other aspects of the entity's identity are firmly grounded in two of the most influential subgenres in horror cinema: zombies and slashers.

A product of mythology surrounding Haitian voodoo after the overthrow of the country's French occupiers, zombies entered the US cinematic vernacular with *White Zombie* (1932) and appeared on the big screen sporadically with few standouts until George A. Romero revitalised the subgenre with his 1968 masterpiece *Night of the Living Dead* (though arguably it was Romero's *Dawn of the Dead* [1978] that would ultimately cement the zombie genre in modern cinema) (Luckhurst, 2015). The concept of the zombie is particularly effective because the roaming dead reveal anxieties, most often in the form of a loss of autonomy and freedom. On a national scope, zombies can represent the mindless banality of capitalism, the monotonous lockstep of modern routine, an overcrowded world bursting at the seams, or even the war-torn streets of a post-9/11 world. In short, zombies resonate as the embodiment of repressed societal anxieties, 'anomalies that straddle crucial cultural boundaries' in that 'they are simply us reflected back, depersonalized, flat-lined by the alienating tedium of modern existence' (Luckhurst, 2015: 10). If the dead walk the earth, and humans who get bitten turn into zombies, the imbalance widely favours those seeking fresh flesh, which contributes to the sense of being overwhelmed and helpless. But these metaphors only work for the mindless, soulless *masses*. Alone, zombies are themselves unthreatening—slow and stupid is no way to go through the afterlife, let alone overtake society. A lone dawdler is someone to pity, maybe even commiserate, but not fear. Individually, these beings are easily dispatched. You can defeat them with a bullet to the head, a banjo to the brain, or even a well-placed golf ball in the cranium. It's the numbers that generate terror; a herd is overwhelming, a harbinger of things to come, while the individual could be little more than an inconvenience—hardly a focal point for an entire film.

Like any strong concept, the zombie universe is governed by rules, and like any structured universe imagined and constructed by creative artists, some of these rules are broken, often even by notable entries. However, even then it's only one or two rules at a time, lest it cease to remain a zombie movie. Some are relatively minor changes—the zombies in *Dawn of the Dead* are blue for some reason—while others are more significant; *Day of the Dead* (1985) lays the groundwork for the zombie revolt in *Land of the Dead* (2005), with scientists demonstrating techniques for training the undead and triggering memories of learned behaviours, such as shaving. But despite the inconsistencies, zombies follow rules.[3] For instance, humans cannot turn into zombies and then turn back into humans; it'd be pretty unfair to come back from the dead twice. Other rules are (for the most part) canonical, and play an important role in constructing the entity.

Zombies rarely possess any sort of strategising or long-term reasoning capability, *Land of the Dead*'s Big Daddy and his loyal followers notwithstanding. Crude tools for an immediate gain are acceptable—the first zombie Barbra sees in *Night of the Living Dead* attacks her with a brick—but overall such an act is rare and short-lived; zombies ultimately let their teeth do the talking. Zombies are easily stymied by physical barriers and often are not too smart; it's how they get trapped in wells or tricked into obvious traps. Originally, zombies were so braindead that they needed someone in charge.

The monsters in *White Zombie* and other early entries in the zombie filmography are controlled by an overlord of sorts. This approach died with *Night of the Living Dead* and has not been resurrected, likely because a vacuous mob driven solely and relentlessly by a desire to murder and eat (rarely in that order) until no food source remained was ultimately far more horrifying than some rogue manipulating the masses for comparatively benign goals. Likewise, zombies appear to also lack memories or even remnants of the souls of the now-vacated vessels.[4] It's just as well—even if they had something to say, they're incapable of saying it. Zombies also cannot talk, but they can moan, groan and hiss-screech as they wander the earth. This inability to speak reminds us that they cannot be reasoned with, that they are truly sub-human with only the most innate of agendas. Again, for a lone zombie this is troubling, but witnessing a herd descending on castaways with the single-mindedness of a hive mind with no communication or coordination is particularly disconcerting.

Zombies walk or shuffle, at least until recently. The introduction of the rage virus in *28 Days Later* (2002), the 'mad cow burger' in *Zombieland* (2009), and the generic virus of *World War Z* (2013) each gave the zombie-verse some leeway on the whole walking thing, resulting in a surprising schism amongst fans. Actor Simon Pegg, star of the terrific *Shaun of the Dead* (2004), famously penned a column for the *Guardian* to discuss his strong feelings on the subject:

> ZOMBIES DON'T RUN! I know it is absurd to debate the rules of a reality that does not exist, but this genuinely irks me. You cannot kill a vampire with an MDF stake; werewolves can't fly; zombies do not run. It's a misconception, a bastardisation that diminishes a classic movie monster. The best phantasmagoria uses reality to render the inconceivable conceivable. The speedy zombie seems implausible to me, even within the fantastic realm it inhabits. A biological agent, I'll buy. Some sort of super-virus? Sure, why not. But death? Death is a disability, not a superpower. It's hard to run with a cold, let alone the most debilitating malady of them all. (Pegg, 2008)

Regardless of the controversy, the classic zombie model is firmly in the slow-but-steady-eats-the-face philosophy. This slow-moving adversary seems benign—avoid the zombie by walking slightly faster seems like the obvious solution—but it's surprisingly effective, thanks in large part to their numbers. Their slow pace carries with it a deceptively effective device for generating fear, its plodding inevitability underscoring the futility of escape. People tire, they need to stop to eat, sleep, or simply catch their breath. Zombies just keep going until they don't have to go any more.

Finally, every creature has a weakness, be it an exorcism for the possessed, electricity for most monsters, or any number of stabbing implements for serial killers. Even something that cannot be killed typically has a way of being contained, like boxing up the blob after battling Steve McQueen and depositing it in the Arctic. Thankfully, zombies can be killed (again), but the only way to do so is by destroying what's left of its mind. From the county sheriff in *Dawn* to the newscaster in *Shaun*, eventually someone explains that zombies 'go down permanently when you shoot them in the head', which is why they only can be stopped by 'removing the head or destroying the brain'.

In *It Follows*, the entity borrows many of the zombie rules. In a nod to traditional (Pegg might say authentic) zombie lore, the entity does not accelerate beyond a walk. Whether it's the old woman on campus or Yara's twin on the beach, the entity moves (for the most part) at the same pace. Two of the entity's forms do appear to move slightly faster than the others: the speed-walking Greg imitation that ultimately kills (the real) Greg, and the tall man whose long stride allows him to move quickly down the halls of Jay's house. However, they're still walking, and at no point does the entity appear to alter its speed upon approaching a victim. This aforementioned inevitability is even more horrifying than the standard zombie straggler. When the pursued stops to stave off exhaustion, the entity is still walking toward her, gaining ground. The victim understands this, resulting in a sense of urgency (not to mention the accompanying anxiety) that never disappears. This is why Jay barricades herself in her room, this is why even after the entity is 'killed' in the pool, there's no respite; she's still lying at the edge of her bed, staring vacantly into space. Even when the entity isn't there, it is.

An earlier version of the script shows that at least one iteration of the entity can make noise, but nothing like that remains in the actual film (more on this in a minute). Overall, communication is something the entity seems either unable to do, or is uninterested in. Likewise, as per Hugh's description, the entity is 'not stupid', while zombies typically are. In fact, the only other trait the entity shares with zombies is the weakness, but it's a big one: the headshot. Once Greg adds a gun to the equation, the entity is hit multiple times with bullets—impressive given its invisibility—but until the last shot, it's only ever slowed, never stopped. Jay shoots the entity in Yara's form in the neck and it falls to the ground, but immediately stands back up. Paul's shot to the back of the head knocks the entity into the pool, but it starts to drown Jay. Ultimately, it's the bullet to the top of the head that causes the entity to disappear, at least for a while. While it can be slowed temporarily by a shot to the crown of the head, it seems to be immune to everything else. It's been posited that the entity's weakness is water, which is an intriguing theory. After all, Jay's entity-father walks along the edge of the pool without jumping in, and when Jay and Paul are having sex, the camera zooms in on the window where we can see the rain pouring outside, suggesting that the two might be safe in that moment. However, I dismiss that theory, as it's pouring with rain outside the natatorium when the entity reaches the group, and while the entity seemed oddly reluctant to dive into the water after her, when it did fall into the water following Paul's execution-style shot, it wasn't trying to flee or flail about; it almost drowns Jay until being struck atop the head by another bullet. It's just as likely its disappearance in the pool ultimately led to the entity's hiatus while Paul and Jay consummated their love.

A zombie has weaknesses—its vulnerability, lack of mobility, inability to reason—which is why Mitchell supplements those characteristics with attributes from the slasher subgenre to compensate. In these films, despite a relatively stable group of stock characters, the most famous is the titular slasher, a (typically) male individual who Sipos describes as having 'a superhuman durability and tenaciousness that sets him beyond mortal control' (2010: 16). Kendrick elaborates on the 'beyond mortal control' aspect by positing that the killer is 'vaguely supernatural to the extent that he appears to have mastery over space and vision that far outstrips that of his victims, allowing him to appear and disappear at will as well as constantly rebuke even the most vigorous attempts to kill him' (2017: 317). This inability to kill the psychotic murderer is one of the key features of the entity; its invisibility (to everyone other than the victim), dogged determination skirting the need to eat or sleep, and rigid code for how (and who) it's passed on to are essential to the entity's being, but the true horror comes from the fact that it cannot be stopped. Any slasher worthy of a franchise returns from the dead again and again.[5] Sequels abound in the horror world, often with the same premise with the same general villain (a new group of unsuspecting victims venturing into the backwoods to encounter new hillbillies in the *Wrong Turn* franchise or radioactive wastelands in the *Hills Have Eyes* franchises); but the originals are dead, defeated at the end of each previous installment. For slasher films, it's the same bloodthirsty guy resurrected somehow.

Slasher films are also notorious for associating sexual acts with murder, with content analyses of slasher films revealing eroticised violence centred around those women who'd had sex. Slashers dole out judgment for intercourse; some are subtle (*Texas Chain Saw Massacre* [1974]) while others are more overt (*Halloween*, *Friday the 13th*). As Clover explained, 'the cause-and-effect relationship between (illicit) sex and death could hardly be more clearly drawn' (2015: 34). That was before *It Follows* came along. Here, the entity also enforces violating sexual mores, and like the slasher, it doesn't differentiate between true love, relationship status, promiscuity or experimentation; Michael Myers doesn't care about Laurie's crush on Ben Tramer, and the entity doesn't care that Paul found love. However, for the entity, the rules are straightforward and unwavering in terms of targeting the latest victim. While the maniac in slasher films targets members of the group beyond those who commit sexual transgressions, the entity is exclusively focused on those on its sexual hit list.

Zombies cannot reason or think, but the Michaels and Jasons of the horror world absolutely can. Michael dons a white sheet to mask his figure—a wise move considering he and Bob were not exactly body doubles—but more eerily, he wears glasses on the outside of the sheet to fool Lynda. It's an unsettling scene, as it demonstrates a cunning instinct to terrify. He could have simply walked into the room and stabbed her (ending her annoying laugh that much sooner), but he wants to savour the realisation, to watch her slowly understand what is happening as confusion morphs into terror. Freddy Krueger torments his victims mercilessly, calling to Nancy as her (deceased) friend Tina and tonguing Nancy through her phone following Johnny Depp's death, hissing that *he's* her boyfriend now.

Like a demented recipe, Mitchell combines these attributes to create a particularly effective foe. As discussed earlier, a draft of the *It Follows* script alluded to attempts by the entity to communicate. As Jay is tied to a wheelchair and the entity walks toward her, the script action reads, 'The woman contorts the muscles in her mouth – oddly –

revealing teeth and tongue.' And a few lines later: 'The middle-aged woman opens her mouth again, straining the muscles in her throat.' However, in the film, only one version of the entity makes a noise: the boy in the boathouse. He practically unhinges his jaw to let out an unearthly scream, reminiscent of the pod people in the *Invasion of the Body Snatchers* (1978). However, while it appears that Jay can hear him, her friends do not react to the noise. The fear of zombies' inability to speak is that they cannot be reasoned with. Slashers can communicate but most choose not to, making desperate pleas useless; the refusal is next-level unsettling, as it becomes about choice rather than capability. While the entity may not be able to communicate, it is preceded by an ominous sonic boom, much like Jason's infamous *chi chi chi, ha ha ha* or the heavy breathing (and occasional electronic synthesizer trill) when Michael Myers would appear. Like all horror music cues, the booms cannot be heard by any of the characters, but Mitchell wisely holds off on the noise until the audience is certain the approaching individual is an entity.

At first glance, the entity appears to be an emotionless being obeying its raison d'être, but it's surprisingly strategic, which is on display in its ability to transform. Mitchell explained that when placing the entity, he was looking for contrast to heighten the unsettled sense that the threatened character must feel: 'When I wrote those scenes where we see different forms of the monster, I tried to just think about what was troubling to me in each of those situations' (Buchanan, 2015). An old woman wandering across the quad and through a college building while wearing a nightgown is unnatural and unexpected, playing to the contrast Mitchell is trying to harness. But when it's not standing out for effect, it's doing what Hugh observed: Taking the form of someone the victim knows in order to hurt that individual. And that pain is diabolical. Jay offers no spark of awareness when confronting any of the entity's forms, save the one they encounter in the final showdown. This burst of recognition amidst a wave of hysteria ratchets up the discomfort as she grapples with the frighteningly familiar. Ultimately, it's not just Hugh seeing his nude mom walking toward him—which is indisputably creepy—but it's also that the last thing Greg saw before he died was his topless mother straddling him. It's a level of torment that can only be found in the most psychotic of slashers.

Moreover, the entity might not only be taking form for the sake of contrast or suffering. The only version of the entity that is never acknowledged by its characters appears when the gang is investigating Hugh's identity. As Jay and Greg walk into Hugh's old high school to find out his real name from the school yearbook adviser (yet another adult whose face we never see), Mitchell's expert use of the 360° pan reveals a young redhead wearing a white coat. The rest of the people in the shot read as "normal"—a couple making out on the ground in the foreground, two students talking to one another in the distance—but everyone is either still or walking away. The girl in the white coat is walking toward the camera, starting out directly in front of a wall with no door. When the camera swings around again, she's again the only one still walking toward the camera, ignoring the sidewalk and staring straight ahead. She's close enough that we can see her carrying a backpack slung over one shoulder. Again, Jay never acknowledges seeing her, but before Greg and Jay drive away (while Paul stares longingly in the backseat), Mitchell uses rack focus to draw attention through the windshield of the redhead walking directly toward the car in the distance.

Again, this is the only iteration of the entity that goes unnoticed and unmentioned. Every other form the entity takes is either meaningful, disturbing or overtly unsettling, with some, such as Jay's emotionless, deceased father, embodying both. The backpacked redhead is subtly threatening because it's the only time we see the entity appearing to attempt to blend in. This betrays a level of cunning normally reserved for psycho-killers. The entity may be subtle in some respects—most notably, its silence and human form—but its purpose appears to be carrying out a mission/death sentence with occasional torment to inflict additional psychological trauma. At no point does the entity fear its quarry is escaping, hence its reluctance to strategise or accelerate beyond a walk. So why don a student disguise after a previous school encounter showed no such propensity for disguise? Most likely, the entity is hiding in plain sight simply to buck a trend. In other words, if the victim realises the entity is always going to be something extremely familiar or completely unexpected, that person will likely train themselves to look for an aberration. Here, the entity is doing something completely unexpected by appearing as normal as possible, hoping to further antagonise its prey.

This behaviour further reinforces the entity's mindset when Jay bursts out of the boathouse after the young boy climbs through the other door. She sprints out of frame just in time to see a young brunette exit the building, wearing a white dress with her curly hair pulled back. We only see her clearly for about four seconds, after which

Jay drives away in Greg's car. Despite the brevity of the encounter, the audience may recognise her from the beginning of the film: it's Annie, hair brushed back and wearing a different outfit, but definitely her. This suggests that the entity might only be able to appear either as someone the victim knows or someone that the entity has killed. The other forms it takes suggests there might be merit to this, as most appear either in some form of physical distress or exhaustion.

From what we see in the rest of the film, this isn't like the T-1000 from *Terminator 2* (1991) running through each of its forms to see if any identities it took would prevent it from drowning in liquid metal; we see it replicate loved ones and we see it replicate strangers, depending on the goal it's trying to accomplish. Jay's first encounter with an entity is with an au naturel version of Hugh's mother, and the two are reintroduced later, corroborating Hugh's warnings of the entity taking the form of the disturbingly familiar. The next time Jay sees a version of the entity that she recognises, it's Yara—in case the audience doesn't recognise her, the real Yara is standing behind a cowering Jay for reference. The only other time Jay notices a familiar manifestation is the final entity: her father. The audience only learns this after the camera focuses on an old family photo. Changing forms into Annie is something really only for the audience to appreciate. As far as the entity is concerned, there's no need to appear in her form. There's no reason not to remain as Yara or the shrieking boy without having to shift its shape. No indicator exists that the entity has to change form after a set amount of time, and since we catch a brief glimpse of the tall man walking by a window of the boathouse, we know that it can repeat forms. From a strategic standpoint, Annie doesn't physically move faster, as we saw with the tall man (longer stride) or (speed-walking) Greg. And Jay doesn't know Annie, so her form serves no tactical advantage to get closer to her.

Granted, there are slight inconsistencies in the entity's mythos, which in itself only enhances the brilliance. For example, almost every one of the entity's forms appeared either nude or wearing white; the woman in Jay's kitchen was wearing a red miniskirt and one white sock with green stripes, but otherwise the appearances were (in order, excluding her): nude, white nightgown, white t-shirt, white jacket, white tank top, white tank top, white dress, white long johns, white nightgown, nude and white tank top. When Jay and her friends are investigating Hugh's abandoned home, they find a sparse closet with two lone shirts hanging up—one black and one white—which could suggest

Hugh knows on some level his end is inevitable. Same for Paul, who in the final scene is clad in a bright white hoodie. Yet, lest too many conclusions be drawn, earlier in the film, when playing the trade game, Hugh asks Jay if she wants to trade places with 'the girl in the yellow dress', who is apparently walking down the aisle of the movie theatre. Hugh might see the entity differently than other victims—with the white outfits tailored to Jay's experience—perhaps to keep any one victim from creating a profile for future targets. Or Hugh's girl in the yellow dress might simply be an exception, a la Jay's girl in the kitchen.

Zombies lack a soul, the once-present light in the eyes of their host bodies, and at first glance, the entity is equally mindless. One discrepancy hints at a deeper level of entity nuance during the brief but meaningful encounter with Greg's mom. The film foreshadows her uniqueness, as she's one of only two non-entity parents whose faces appear in the film; both end up having their form taken by the entity. As Jay races up the stairs, she shouts for Greg to watch out, only to see Mrs. Hannigan wearing a white satin robe and pounding on the door, the thumping reverberating through the house. Jay stares at Mrs. Hannigan relentlessly working to gain entry when Greg's mom stops, turns her head, and locks eyes with Jay. At no other point in the film does an entity acknowledge the presence of anyone other than its target; even when Paul is firing point-blank at Jay's father, the closest thing he does to acknowledging the threat is aimlessly stick his hand back, eyes still locked on Jay. Mrs. Hannigan does know Jay, which might explain the recognition; after all, most forms the entity takes don't apply to anyone else nearby because only the victim could see its form anyway. That said, when the entity was Hugh's mom in the abandoned building, it didn't acknowledge her son; likewise, Jay's father never even glances at Kelly during the swimming pool confrontation. Again, it's that uncertainty that suggests even more rules we are unaware of, rules that likely could only be established after a longer pursuit, though it would mean having to survive that much longer. Given that the entity already pulls its qualities from the supernatural, zombies and slashers—three of the largest, most sustainable subgenres in all of horror—the odds of such an extended run are painfully low.

FOOTNOTES

1. Mitchell says the actor is actually the second tallest man in the world and describes him as a 'super nice guy' (Kirk, 2015).

2. The final scene featuring what may or may not be the entity is not included because of its ambiguity.

3. *Warm Bodies* (2013) is an exception to most of these rules, though the entire premise of the film rests on violating our expectations of zombies (not to mention the entire subclass of zombies in the film that turn out to be the real enemy).

4. The first season of *The Walking Dead* toyed with how much humanity remains in the so-called 'walkers', though this direction was (unfortunately) abandoned a few episodes in.

5. A technical exception would be *Friday the 13th*, in which a few different psychopaths donned the hockey mask, but only after Jason carried the machete for films 2-4.

CHAPTER 3: WHERE GOES THE NEIGHBOURHOOD?

One of the reviews of *It Follows* from a local paper in Detroit described the film's surroundings as being, 'disorienting but well-suited to the local landscape, with Ferndale and Berkley's ranch-style homes, the crumbling ice cream stand on 12 Mile Road, and the Redford Theatre erasing any nostalgia for the past while accenting the divide between decaying Detroit and bland suburbia' (Meyers, 2015). The fact that the events of *It Follows* play out against the wealth divide of Detroit was a key part of Mitchell's original vision. Co-founder of Animal Kingdom—the studio that produced *It Follows*—David Kaplan recalled that when Mitchell pitched the film, 'He had a vision', and that vision 'showed Detroit as the character looming large over the film.' "It was ruin porn, or the city as it exists today'" (Buder, 2015). Mitchell confirmed the importance of the city, which was also the site of *The Myth of the American Sleepover*. Mitchell grew up in the suburbs of Detroit, and says his parents still live there. He still finds himself drawn to the city:

> It's a place where there's a division in terms of race and wealth. Again, I'm not trying to make this sort of grand political statement, but it's a shitty thing. There's no nice way of putting it. It's something that people there are aware of, and it's always seemed strange to me. I felt it was important to show that contrast. It's just a way of hinting at something that I think is very unfortunate. (Nastasi, 2015)

Detroit has long been known for its economic decline, with the city losing over a quarter of a million people between 2000 and 2010 and half its entire population since 1950 (Florida, 2013). Isolated pockets of rejuvenation call to mind Brian Berry's phrase, 'islands of renewal in seas of decay'. Laura Reese and her co-authors of the brilliantly-titled article, "'It's safe to come, we've got lattes": Development disparities in Detroit' describe a city experiencing a steep decline in employment and investment, leaving behind a 'post-apocalyptic neighborhood landscape' (2017: 367). Less than ideal for a city that Frank Bruni called a 'gauge of our soul' (2015).

Don't Breathe—which coincidentally also took place in Detroit—flirted with discussing poverty, but the housing blight was only a hasty explanation for why screams might go unheard. Apart from an establishing shot of the only mowed lawn on the block, the movie pays its surroundings no heed. Other horror films discuss urban poverty, such as *The People Under the Stairs* (1991) and *Candyman* (1992), though the bold satire of the former and the racial themes of the latter garner most of the attention. In terms of focusing on class and the city, the closest film to *It Follows* was *Judgment Night* (1993), perfectly summarised by the *AV Club* as, 'Emilio Estevez and Cuba Gooding Jr. playing yuppies stranded in a bad area and on the run from, seriously, gang leader Denis Leary.' That film opens on the most tranquil suburbia this side of Pleasantville, complete with kids on bikes, and neighbours out walking and working on their cars, all while autumn leaves swirl around them. Six minutes later, the quartet is driving their outlandish RV through a dark, deserted ghetto, the fluttering leaves now replaced with a whirlwind of discarded newspapers dancing across the frame. The clunky but well-meaning dialogue echoes this juxtaposition, skirting '90s-era racist statements for surprisingly introspective empathy: when Jeremy Piven scoffs at the suggestion that the downtown residents could be his neighbours, Estevez counters with the realisation that they live less than ten miles away. But *Judgment Night* was an outlier, and the horror genre continued to give discussions of class a wide berth.[1]

Before we explore this further, it's incredibly difficult to separate issues of class and race in US horror, as talking about one inevitably (and rightfully) raises questions about the other. However, here the discussion of race is absent because of the uniformity of the suburbs (and therefore the cast). The 'invisible flexibility'[2] of Whiteness allows for a film to take place near one of the largest Black metropolitan centres in the country and yet have only a handful of people of colour on-screen.[3] And yet, that's kind of the point. In the de-facto segregated suburbs, interpersonal networks dictate uniformity of a group of friends who have grown up together, and that's likely what Mitchell was aiming to accomplish. Like in *Sleepover*, the lack of diversity not only adds to the realism, but also drives home the point of how these two worlds exist only miles apart. But while the racial uniformity does not lend itself to an interrogation of racial dynamics, the geographical journey through the manicured and tattered landscapes of the city showcases the pronounced socio-economic divides in a way this is stunningly effective.

This avoidance of inequality is due to a variety of issues—not the least of which is a nationwide tendency to shy away from such discussions—but practicality factors in prominently. Horror movies are typically sound investments, and so due to cost effectiveness and scheduling restrictions, horror movies tend to hunker down once they reach an area, be it the outpost in *The Thing* (1982), the makeshift town in the *House of Wax* (2005) remake, the forest in *The Forest* (2016), or house and grounds in *Get Out* (2017). Being trapped is frightening, and the familiarity of a particular location allows the suspense to build as the audience becomes familiar with its spatial geography. However, single locations often make a comparison between the privileged and the under-privileged difficult; instead of examining the balance of inequality, we see one extreme or the other.

For example, squalour is a horror mainstay, a form of otherness that feels hopeless while allowing for plausible explanations as to why help is not on the way. The dilapidated lair in *Texas Chain Saw Massacre* or the ramshackle hut in *Wrong Turn* (2003) are extreme sites of destitution, providing an other-worldly locale foreign enough to be disturbing, yet close enough to be plausibly threatening; an alien location buried in the darkness just off a lonely highway. On the other end of the spectrum is the wealthy demographic, the sisters on *Sorority Row* (2009) or club members of *The In-Crowd* (2000). However, they're not shown juxtaposed with one another, apart from some relatable main character's monologue about how different this place is from 'back home'. To that end, class can sometimes be used as a convenient avenue for character development, an efficient way of establishing motivations through broad generalisations behind class backgrounds. This is a popular approach because it also provides a fish-out-of-water protagonist to whom rules, rituals and urban legends must be explained. The son of an impoverished fisherman in *I Know What You Did Last Summer* (1997), the high school senior transplant to Cradle Bay in *Disturbing Behaviour* (1998), a poor graduate student in *You're Next* (2011)—each calls attention to the strangeness of the uniqueness of their place on the social ladder. However, simply having a character who is rich or poor no more makes a film 'about' class than having a Black or Asian character makes it 'about' race.

It Follows does brave an overt discussion of the city and its differences. For their ill-fated final plan, the gang drives deeper into Detroit, once again passing rows of dilapidated homes. Walking the final stretch to the natatorium, we see more homes in disrepair, with crumbling staircases and chipped paint. Jay stares up at one of them as she walks by, a massive brick house, front porch collapsed and windows boarded up while eviction notices hang on the doors. Yara recalls:

> When I was a little girl, my parents told me I wasn't allowed to go south of 8 Mile. I didn't even understand what that meant. It wasn't until I got a little older that I realised that was where the city started and the suburbs ended. I started thinking how weird and shitty that was. I had to ask permission to go to the state fair with my best friend and her parents just because it was a few blocks past the border.

As it turns out, Yara likely has a built-in excuse for being shot in the leg. Judging by Paul's presence as Yara tips back a container of Jello in the hospital, it's likely that the story was they ventured south of 8 Mile and that's how she got injured.

More than a single monologue, however, are the status markers placed throughout the film, though it's the strategic use of neighbourhoods that tells the story. In the opening scene, before doomed Annie emerges from her house, the camera sits in the middle of the street, the road stretching endlessly towards the horizon. The houses are set so far back off of the street that the front porches are barely visible, nestled back amongst mature maples, oaks and elms. Crisp concrete curbs and sidewalks frame the shot, with autumn colours standing out against the falling dusk light. We will see this shot repeatedly throughout the film, each denoting a different neighbourhood, a different level of status for its residents.

A quiet street in Annie's neighbourhood.

The Height home is still in the suburbs—Jay's walk home with Kelly shows the same manicured lawns, but on much smaller lots, with small, single-story brick homes speckled with siding that sit closer to the narrower concrete roads. They live in one of the few two-story homes on the block, but the Height house betrays status markers that separate it from Annie's neighbourhood, reminding us of Jay's place in this world: the above-ground pool, the slow pan across the chain link fence separating their home from the neighbours, four flimsy plastic lawn chairs on the thin strip of patio.

Jay and Kelly walk down a street in their neighbourhood.

The search for Hugh takes them deeper into Detroit. Shots on the drive down there show abandoned building after abandoned building, the bare brick walls and plywood-covered windows dotted with graffiti. This isn't idle stock footage to pad out the runtime; Mitchell cuts back to Jay staring out the car window three separate times, staring intently at the deteriorating landscape. Just as we saw a clean wide shot from the middle of the street for Annie's and Jay's homes, we get the identical shot as they're driving. Here, the houses are large, but old, and the shot feels claustrophobic by comparison as the front yards are almost nonexistent. Porches and roofs show wear and disrepair, while the darker, asphalt road sporadically lined with grown (but not mature) trees is speckled with errant litter, piles of leaves, and the occasional garbage can.

Once Jay and her crew finally track down Hugh's mother's house, it's in a wealthy neighbourhood. The two-story homes are all set far back from the wide, bright concrete streets on neatly trimmed yards peppered with mature blue spruces and the occasional basketball hoop. What's most prevalent, however, is the *space*. The street is deserted, and the wide-angle shot down the block accentuates the size of the lawns and how far apart the houses are from one another. When Jay and her friends confront Hugh, they're sitting in his backyard, which backs up to a soccer field, further underscoring the space.

Downtown neighbourhood.

In a film about having room to evade an unstoppable entity, there is a direct relationship between the number of options and amount of available space.

A spacious street in Hugh's neighbourhood.

Hugh is acutely aware of space, frantically telling Jay and her friends, 'We shouldn't be in the same place. You need to get the fuck out of here!' And when Hugh is providing more specifics about the entity to Jay and her friends, he reminds her, 'Wherever you are, it's somewhere walking straight for you… but it is *walking*. If you drive far enough, you can buy yourself some time…' This concept of distance is key, as this tangible limitation informs the victim's strategy. But what is left unsaid is the social distance, the space that can only be measured by status, not location. Hugh chooses to infect someone who is not on his social plane. At least on some level, Hugh understood the importance of this social separation. This is likely why he targeted Jay: she's close enough to share interests and experiences, which likely makes it easier to seduce her, but they're not likely to run into each other at school, work or a social gathering.

Greg does not understand this concept, or at the very least ignores it. Given the amount of time that passes and the shot of Greg flirting with a freshman at the student union cafeteria over a burger and fries, we can assume he slept with someone else, marking the next victim. This explains how, when Paul, Kelly and Yara ask him if he's seen anything, he could honestly report that he has not. Too late, Greg learns his lesson, but for Jay, we see the ramifications of the intersection of physical and social space after Greg's death. Once he's killed, the entity briskly walks out of the front door on his way to Jay's house, which is just across the street. Here we see the physical manifestation of the consequences of proximity. Jay ultimately chooses companionship over logic when she sleeps with Paul, but Paul's behaviour after intercourse suggests some level of understanding, either of his own or of a plan they developed together. Paul chooses to pass the entity across class lines, crawling for prostitutes in a desolate area of town, eyeing women who, based solely on attire, typically deal with a class of clientele without means.

Paul's solution is not ideal, but it's a product of inequality and a practical solution. The prostitute will likely quickly pass the curse on. Certainly, a number of barriers prevent the victims from escaping the entity. Age is an obvious one—as teens, it's not like they can get transferred to a different office on the other side of the country. But poverty is the subtler, more pervasive barrier. Jay's movement through the film as she tracks Hugh and then evades the entity allows us to see the inequality at different locations in and around her urban environment. Yet in doing so, Jay experiences a Dickensian-esque vision of her own lack of mobility. She starts in the classroom of her community college, essentially alone (save Greg) as her childhood friends have moved away for school. She journeys through a gauntlet of dilapidated ruins to Hugh's abandoned home, seeing firsthand the potential price of independence. She sees Hugh living at home with his mother, reminding her of her own current situation. And through it all,

Jay is accompanied by her fiercely loyal younger sister's friends and her high school ex, reinforcing an emotional separation as well as a slew of physical barriers. When Jay and her friends need to escape, they don't drive to the Detroit Metropolitan Airport to hop a flight to Canada or the coast. Instead they drive to Greg's family home, apparently only a couple of hours away. Once Jay is reminded of the scope of the entity's mindless determination, she grows more and more desperate, culminating in a mad dash from her street to…the middle of a strange forest. Having Jay flee demonstrates the limited scope of her options, as all she sees—all we see—is a dreary landscape from which there is no escape.

The entire concept of disrupting class lines is daunting, but calling attention to economic disparity in a country that rarely discusses such issues—certainly not to the proportion in which they occupy the physical space—adds to the horror of the film. Andrew Tudor argued that 'a recognition that to fracture a naturalistically represented physical order is, simultaneously, to affirm both the precariousness and the significance of that order' (p. 124). Tudor described this as an essential tension in horror movies, and while he was talking about what would be best described as the entity, the structural restrictions of a system that fundamentally restricts options masquerading as the natural order serves as a powerful tool for instilling unease in viewers.

FOOTNOTES

1. Meanwhile, across the Atlantic, British horror films have shown no such reluctance, exploring class in several films, such as *Eden Lake* (2008), *The Disappeared* (2008), and *F* (2010).
2. Linda Flores uses this term to describe the ability of Whiteness to 'move with ease' and 'retains its invisibility and race neutrality' (p. 184), resulting in what Henry Giroux would describe as 'a racial marker, an index of social standing or rank' as it is 'both invisible to itself and at the same time the norm by which everything is measured' (p. 305).
3. The only people of colour clearly visible in the entire film are two boys we see through a hospital window and Jay's teacher lecturing about Lazarus.

CHAPTER 4: 'I NEED WATER!'

The best horror films are saying something more, be it complicated gender politics, nationwide policy decisions, reaction to a significant event, or simply exploring an issue that deserves more attention. Directors rarely complain about how others read their film (unless it's a particularly narrow-minded conclusion), and Mitchell is no different.

> I have no problem with other interpretations. Whether I agree with them or not, and even if they're troubling to me (and I've read some that are), I don't think it's my place to tell people that they can't analyze the film separate from my intention. (Nastasi, 2015)

It Follows is made for this sort of analysis, particularly as far as the entity is concerned.

The most straightforward interpretation is that the entity represents the spectre of adulthood, one of looming responsibility and grounded dreams. In broad strokes, Jay is already hovering in the limbo twixt teen and adulthood, and her companions are not far behind. Early in the film, after sex with Hugh, Jay openly laments the difficulties surrounding growing up:

> It's funny, I used to daydream about being old enough to go on dates and drive around with friends in their cars. I had this image of myself holding hands with a really cute guy, listening to music on the radio and driving along a pretty road... maybe somewhere up north... after the trees started to change colour. It was never about going anywhere... just having some kind of freedom I guess. Now we're old enough, but where the hell do we go, right?

The details make for a convincing argument as well. After Hugh chloroforms Jay in the backseat, she awakens tied tightly to a wheelchair, unable to tear free. Alone, incapacitated, Jay can only stare ahead as a naked woman in her 40s walks steadily toward her, unwavering and unmerciful, all while a young man shouts instructions on how to avoid her fate. Before Hugh abandons Jay in the middle of the street, we see Yara, Kelly and Paul playing Old Maid on the patio, a game in which the sole purpose is to not get stuck holding the namesake's crude caricature. Kelly holds the losing hand, the old dame's puckered lips and exaggerated wrinkles in sharp contrast to Kelly's flamingo thumb ring and black nail polish. The never-married elderly woman is a 'stock character' in the US, 'a metaphor for barrenness, ugliness, and death' and this 'obvious undesirability' is replicated and reinforced in the card game (Simon, 1987: 2).

After Yara quotes Dostoyevsky, Paul asks Kelly if her mom is asleep. Kelly assures her, explaining that Mrs. Height wakes up at 5:15, adding, 'I think that would kill me'. Mrs. Height gets a rare parental mention in the movie, but not much beyond that, which isn't necessarily an aberration for the genre; parents were almost completely absent from *Halloween*. Mitchell's previous (and first) film also lacked parental intervention and guidance, so much so that A.O. Scott posited that the unseen parents in the *Myth of the American Sleepover* were actually the Detroit suburb teens from *Freaks and Geeks* all grown up. The parental absence in *It Follows* was another connection to *Sleepover*, a link so apparent that after Mitchell's editor read the script for *It Follows*, he said, 'This is like a nightmare sequel to your first movie!' With the parents almost completely absent in *Sleepover*, they cede the screen to their offspring to create a world as only teens can see it: theirs and theirs alone. Here, parents are visible, but—quite literally—just barely. We never once see the full face of Jay and Kelly's mother. The first time we see her, she's at the table talking on the phone, and all we can see is the back of her head. This will largely be her role for the rest of the film: hiding in plain sight.

The entity takes the form of adults, but as for the rest of the world, only two parents' faces are clearly visible in this film. First, we see Greg's mom talking with her son as they stare out of a large picture window onto the melee of flickering police lights and curious bystanders; the next time we see her, she is pounding on the door of Greg's room—the entity in disguise—after which she mounts her son and drains the life from him. The other adult who speaks (and who is visible when that rare feat occurs) is when Jay opens the door to Hugh's home only to see his mother, Mrs. Redmond. The last time Jay saw her, Mrs. Redmond was nude, walking toward Jay as she struggled to free herself from the chair. You can see the look of realisation on Jay's face when Mrs. Redmond opens the door; similarly, Hugh had stared in awed horror at his nude mother at the abandoned warehouse. Those two adults are granted facetime, but even then only to play on the horror of recognition. The rest are faceless cyphers of a world representing responsibility and burden, one of long work hours, divorce and death.

And it's not as though Mitchell is demonising the mother, or any other parent for that matter. There's no imagery of her drinking herself to sleep; *Elm Street*'s Marge Thompson practically lived in an inebriated state, endangering her daughter who was trapped in a nightmare.[1] By all visual accounts, Mrs. Height is a single mom who tries to be there for her kids.[2] After Jay's car accident, we see her mother (face partially off-screen) fast asleep on a chair in Jay's hospital room, arm wrapped around her other daughter Kelly with Yara slumped against both of them. She's not around to keep them from gallivanting off to Greg's lake house or skirting south of 8 Mile to break into a natatorium after hours. Mitchell explains this technique was deliberate:

> The fact that you rarely see any of the parents or adults in the film, they're on the edge of the frame or they're barely there, all of that is to suggest something that doesn't feel quite right, that is a little bit outside of reality or the way that we see the world. (Crump, 2015)

This approach is effective. In *Sleepover*, mothers and/or fathers are gone so that teens can experience true independence, free from the meddling, judgmental eyes of their parents. And in *Follows*, it's not just parents. We only see Jay's side of the conversation with the police officer, the faces of the paramedics blurry in the background. We see police officers again in a wide shot in front of the dilapidated building, but they're set further back in the shot and the darkness of dusk keeps them relatively anonymous. But while this anonymity could be a teenager's dream, it has the opposite effect in *It Follows*. Here, the absence of adults is not only the absence of authorities but also the absence of *authority*, embodying the uncertainty felt during those difficult years between adolescence and adulthood. The experience is indicative of where these characters are in their lives, approaching a time when parental advice is no longer a source of eye-rolling defiance, but rather something to be appreciated, even occasionally followed—at least to an extent. For Mitchell, the absence is neither malicious nor indifferent, merely a device for involuntary independence.

The age issue seems to orbit Jay as well. Early on in the film, Jay is playing the 'trade game' with Hugh, where one person has to identify someone to trade lives with, and the other person has to guess. Jay incorrectly guesses that Hugh would want to swap with a 20-something guy making out with an attractive blonde, but he surprises her by saying he would rather be the young boy nearby. Asked why, Hugh simply replies, 'How cool would it be to have your whole life ahead of you?' Dark for a 21-year-old, but it's a precursor to when Jay begins to regress herself. When Jay is talking to Paul and Kelly about her encounter at school with the entity in geriatric form, she's picking at her small bowl of ice cream—chocolate swirl with sprinkles—like a young child. The first time the entity enters her house, Jay flees to a swing set at a nearby park. Even after temporarily defeating the entity in the pool (and the ensuing intercourse with Paul), Jay lays in her bed, comforted by her mom.

Throughout the film, Jay takes in her surroundings through a seemingly inconsequential but uniquely youthful activity: staring up at the sky. Mitchell establishes this shot early with Jay floating on her back in her backyard pool, staring up at patches of cumulus clouds against a deep blue sky, hovering beyond the distant branches of mature trees swaying in the wind. The shot doesn't last long—barely four seconds—yet it captures a fleeting moment of relaxation, comfort, sanctuary and hope. Unfortunately for Jay, this is the last time we see this moment of clarity.

After Jay encounters the entity in her home, she grabs a kid's bike, *Goonies* (1985) style, and rides to the nearest park. There she sits on a swing, alone, slowly moving her bare feet through the sand, pushing herself slowly back and forth but never breaking contact with the relative safety of the ground. The park after dark has a lifeless, unnatural feel, particularly for a site of whimsical joy and youth. She looks in several different directions for the entity, and likely for help, but she is faced with stony silence. While surveying the perimeter and kneading the sand with her toes, Jay again looks up at the sky. This time, she's met with darkness, a starless void flattening what should be a limitless look upward and forward.

The next time we see her look up is again at night, this time from the hood of her car after witnessing Greg's death. Again, blackness overshadows everything else, with a hint of tree leaves and branches at the periphery. Upon waking the next morning, Jay rolls on her back and looks up, this time greeted with a cloudless but muted sky. Trees still form a boundary, framing the patch of pale blue sky, but they're younger trees that lack the towering expanse of her first glance upward, and now bare, leafless branches beneath the canopy reach out like claws, the tendrils grasping at her.

Jay's view from her swimming pool.

Jay's view of the night sky from a swingset in the park.

Jay's view of the sky from the hood of her car.

The comfort of the view from her pool is now a distant memory. Staring up at the sky is a manifestation of hope and curiosity, of looking forward to the future and the unknown rather than grousing about current problems or past mistakes. But that sanctuary is gone now; there's no more time for daydreams.[3] It's worth noting here when such a shot does *not* appear in the film, such as when Jay was wading around her pool after breaking her wrist in the car wreck. She walks to the edge of the pool, dry torso and hair, careful to keep her cast out of the water. There she leans against the side of the pool and stares intently toward the corner of her house, gazing to see who or what would be walking through the gate. This shot mirrors the opening scene with Jay, but her demeanour is completely different, shrouded in unease and melancholy: a wholly anhedonic experience.

In the rare instance that Mitchell discusses meaning behind his decisions, he has alluded to age:

> To me, it's more about sex being a normal part of life. It's the act of living that opens us up to danger. It's not just about sex. It's about life. It's about dealing with mortality. I'm not denying there is a way of reading it. Maybe a preferred interpretation for me would just be: it's the fear, at that age, of what that means and what you imagine that experience to be, and the fears that are connected. The fears of becoming an adult and entering the world, and all the things that follow that.

But it's more than just about growing old in suburbia with a mortgage, great schools, and likely opioid addiction. The frequent, mindful use of water imagery in *It Follows* builds on this idea of a fear of aging in a more nuanced way. In the prologue, we see a desperate Annie on the run from an as-yet-unseen force. She frantically drives away, attempting to put some distance between her and the entity. Ultimately, however, she stops at the shoreline and waits for a gruesome death slowly walking toward her. It's possible the spot has emotional significance; when Jay had sex with Hugh, they were making out on a blanket sitting on a rocky beach until Jay suggested they go back to the car. Regardless, for Annie, the water serves as a last stop, the backdrop of a final apologetic phone call to her parents, the physical end of her doomed journey.

The entity itself has an unclear relationship with water. As discussed, it's not an outright weakness per se, but something worth unpacking. The entity seems reluctant to enter water. Upon entering the natatorium and surveying Paul's horribly-flawed plan, the entity begins hurtling objects rather than enter the water. Again, it cannot stop the entity, but water does seem to slow it down. And yet, water also plays a part in how the entity kills its victims. The first of only two deaths is shown at the beginning of the film following Annie's apologetic, resigned farewell phone call to her parents. A hard cut to the next morning reveals her lifeless eyes and torso, her waistline partially submerged in a shallow pool of water bordered by lighter, dry sand. It's not blood—the next shot reveals bright red stains streaked across the sand by her legs, the carnage contrasted with the peaceful lake at dusk in the background. The presence of the puddle is explained following Greg's death, when the entity (now in the form of Greg's mom) is riding atop her son, her crotch secreting a clear viscous liquid that seems to drain his life force.

But it's Jay who most directly struggles with water. Following Annie's death, the next scene opens with Jay floating on her back in her above-ground pool, immersed and at peace. Walking toward the edge of a pool, she notices a small red ant crawling across her arm. She dispels the (very minor) threat by slowly lowering her arm into the pool, the water closing in around her skin to trap the ant before drowning the insect; the victim never realised the extent of what was happening until it was too late, an apt metaphor Jay likely grasps too late. Water continues its symbolic recurrence, at first in an unobtrusive way. While getting ready for her movie date with Hugh, she swallows an unidentified pill without using water. Lest this be confused with an insignificant act, the script calls specifically for this detail: 'She opens the plastic container, pops out a pill and swallows it. *No water necessary*' (emphasis added). On their next date, the couple makes out with the steady lapping of tiny waves in the background, similar to what we heard before Annie's death. After Hugh's assault on Jay, she inspects her body in the mirror, peering down at her crotch before leaning over to take a long drink directly from the running faucet.

After Jay's encounter with Hugh, water unexpectedly takes on a more ominous role. The first form the entity takes when in Jay's kitchen is urinating down her legs, pooling on the floor as she walks. A close-up shot shows the slow cadence, the gurgling squish of each step as an uneven stream splashes down between her feet. Frantic, Jay sprints upstairs, breathlessly slamming the door behind her. She reluctantly lets her sister and Paul inside, and after Kelly suggests sitting down, Jay begins to hyperventilate, shouting, 'I need water!

Oh my God I need water!' From this point forward, Jay uses water to seek comfort, solace for the ongoing, worsening struggle she's enduring, only to no avail. She's further hampered by the effects of the car wreck; even when she was able to climb into her pool, she could never get completely cleansed because casts and water don't mix. Not only is she unable to submerge herself, water becomes a barrier, penning her in with each escape attempt: the gang's trip to the lake house, Jay's sojourn to the woods (when she sees the men in the boat). In the case of the latter, we see a wobbly Jay slowly wade calf-deep into the cold water, but what we don't see is what the script called for when Jay was contemplating swimming out to the boat:

> Her eyes show melancholy as she paddles in place. I can't do this. Jay exhales and drops down into the water. She's gone. We sit on the surface of the lake watching the young men on the boat drink and laugh. Eventually, they start the engine and cruise off along the horizon. A flock of birds flies overhead. The water is still. Jay pops up several yards away—nearly out of frame—gasping for air. She fights to swim back.

This could easily be seen as a suicide attempt; she did just spend a restless night alone having witnessed her one-man entity blockade brutally murdered in front of her, and that glimpse of a future is enough to have anyone contemplate ending a life of constant evasion. However, given the struggle with water, here we see a proposed sequence depicting the water physically rejecting her, Jay rising to the surface as though she'd been spat out. Moreover, Jay struggling to swim back seems odd—it's a lake, not the ocean's undertow, and Jay spends too much time in her pool not to be a skilled swimmer. The problem is the water itself, unable to accept Jay.

Water has long served as a metaphor for rebirth, a reawakening experience of starting anew, refreshed and rejuvenated. However, this isn't about recapturing youth per se; the only lamenting of misspent youth by characters are when Hugh and Jay joke that children can shit wherever and whenever they want to. Simply put, at 21 years old, there's not much to recapture. The fear here isn't the existential dread of getting older with youth inexorably slipping away.

It's not about dying. Like everything else in the movie, it's about sex; rather, it's about the fixation in this film returning to a time when they didn't have to worry about sex. The culprit is not sex per se, but rather the immense hold it has over them, particularly at this point in their lives. *It Follows* explores this fusion of sex and age, and the realisation that the two are inextricably linked. Even beyond Jay's struggles, sex permeates the film. Early in the film, we see two young neighbour boys spying on Jay while she swims; bemused, she says 'I see you' and they duck back down behind the fence—but they don't leave. Later, we see one of the boys outdoors, crouched beneath her bathroom window.[4] Kelly checks out Greg while washing his car, Greg checks out Yara while she's watching Hugh's house, Greg checks out Kelly while she's sunbathing, and Kelly checks Greg out again, all possible thanks to raging adolescent hormones. This undercurrent of sex captures the real fear about age that Mitchell has tapped into: the overpowering sexual confusion these teens are experiencing.

Yara is a great character, but it's Kelly who personifies this. Throughout the film, Kelly is doing her best to protect Jay from harm, which includes everything from Paul's awkward advances to an invisible entity throwing small appliances with astonishing accuracy. Kelly hugs Jay when she's screaming, and we see multiple shots of Kelly with her arms wrapped around Jay as they sleep. These are genuine, instinctive moments between two sisters, demonstrating a deep bond with one another. And yet, on three separate occasions, Kelly shows an interest in Greg. The first is relatively innocuous; when walking home with Jay, talking about her date with Hugh, Kelly sees Greg washing his car and shyly gives a small wave, a slight grin on her face. The second occurs when Greg is driving everyone to his lake house. Unprompted, Kelly tells Greg she appreciates how much he is helping them, and the camera moves in on her entranced as he shares a bit about his childhood, hanging on his every word. She then glances at Jay (who is leaning on Kelly's shoulder) and begins talking with her instead. And finally, on the beach, Greg is drinking beer and not receiving any validation from Jay, despite his repeated attempts at eye contact. Greg then turns his attention to Kelly, who is sunbathing in short-shorts and a revealing strapless bikini top. She catches him glancing at her and turns away, smiling. Greg flat-out stares at Kelly, tipping back the rest of his beer while still checking her out. He then walks away to organically empty some of that beer into nearby reeds as Jay and Kelly *both* watch him leave.

Kelly then looks down, her face betraying slight disappointment, and maybe even some shame. She likely realises that Jay is interested in Greg, ending her chances with him. After all, even a creep like Greg wouldn't date his ex's younger sister; there are rules.

But Kelly had to realise such an action would likely hurt her sister, even when they were riding in the car together. As an adolescent, lust becomes weaponised, and it manifests itself here as the entity. And so, while the entity functions as a stand-in for age, it is not a fear of death or even adulthood, but rather an overwhelming fear of their primal sexual desires as teens. It's a fine line, a very distinct one separating *It Follows* from the heavy-handed morality inherent in slasher films from the more realistic, nuanced approach to understanding and accepting teen sexuality.

This idea of sexuality is likely universal, at least as far as Mitchell intended:

> As far as it being a broader social statement about women and sex, I don't personally see it. It's definitely not my intention. I think it's really more about sex in general. I wouldn't say it's specific to women. (Nastasi, 2015)

Here, I respectfully disagree, as the film moves beyond a static discussion of teens and sex by focusing specifically on women. In other words, we must distinguish between what the entity actually represents and what Jay is experiencing, and her experience is that of a sexual assault victim.

Rape in horror films is often an unspoken fear reinforcing a terrifying situation, though there are subgenres where it's prevalent, most notably rape-revenge films. The rape-revenge subgenre[5] is notorious for disturbing imagery surrounding sexual assault. Such films tend to follow a standard format of stasis (a woman on her own), assault (the woman is raped by one or more assailants), coping (attempting to deal with the trauma), and revenge (undertaken outside traditional legal channels, resulting in death of the attacker). There is some room for resistance to what can be an exploitive batch of films; in a bold departure from other such films, the 2007 film *Teeth* features a woman with a vagina that does the castrating, embodying Barbara Creed's (1993) foundational work on the monstrous feminine, which represents 'what it is about woman that is shocking, terrifying, horrific, abject' (p. 1).

It Follows is immediately set apart from this subgenre because it remains a film where revenge simply cannot be taken.[6] This isn't because of some moral reckoning, a reluctant soul-searching that questions the need for violence. In this case, revenge cannot be taken because it's not an individual who is solely at fault, but rather a much larger system stretching back beyond direct blame. No single culprit was responsible for the entity, there was no ironically doomed soul or maniacal murderer forced to walk the earth for all eternity. Jay could no more fight back against her sexual assault than she could seek vengeance on crime itself. Other such films have danced around this, with the 1981 entry *Ms. 45* (featuring a mute seamstress raped by two different attackers while walking home from work one day) ultimately targeting the patriarchy itself with a male-centric killing spree. But *It Follows* understands better than its peers that the satisfaction of one death or even several deaths rings hollow against the larger, more serious issue of the prevalence of sexual assault. This inability to take revenge—a staple in most cinema involving a gross injustice—shifts the focus to how the victim copes with the trauma. In doing so, the film can challenge preconceived notions surrounding rape.

In her prescient, frighteningly relevant dissection of media coverage about sex crimes, Helen Benedict focused on myths[7] surrounding sexual assault, focusing on the pathology of rape (having the crime motivated by universal inevitabilities that are biological, sociological or cultural in nature), the responsibility of the victim, and the otherness of the assailant. Mitchell begins with the responsibility of the victim by examining consent. Jay is not pressured into sex—she's the one who suggests they go back to the car. However, Hugh misrepresents himself, thereby violating conditional consent; if she had known having sex with him would lead to death, Jay most likely would not have consented to intercourse. This is the distinction that makes 'stealthing'[8] a crime, as does knowingly exposing someone to HIV without their knowledge. When Greg meets Hugh, Greg lashes out, pointedly calling him 'Jeff' to remind everyone that this person had already lied about his identity. In a film where the word 'yes' is spoken just five times, while the word 'no' is spoken 42 times, consent is a constant discussion.

The victim is rarely believed, and Jay is no different. Greg, who defended her in front of Hugh, doesn't believe the danger of the entity itself. When Greg tries to see Jay following her return home from the hospital, he's openly sceptical of her trauma and when Paul insists 'she didn't make it up', Greg responds, 'We'll know sooner or later, right?' Pushed on this statement, Greg simply states, 'Something happened, it's just not what she thinks, okay?'

And Greg's not the only one with doubts. Rape often goes unreported, raising doubts when the police are not contacted. Here, Jay does report the crime, but the authorities are either invisible or worthless; they couldn't even track down Hugh after Jay said she knew where he lived (and subsequently took her friends there). A determined police force would likely solve the crime if the assault had lined up with their preconceived notions of what constitutes rape. Here, Jay is once again left on her own, an ever-expanding chasm between her and the adults who should be helping.

As for the assailant, Hugh's varsity jacket is a red flag in light of recent news stories, but otherwise he's a white male (racist beliefs ensure that people of colour are seen as the most likely and frightening attackers), and he's been on several dates with Jay, as opposed to the more-feared (and vastly less frequent) 'stranger' rape. And by framing his motives as driven by the presence of the entity, it suggests he is not 100 per cent responsible for his actions—but we are entering difficult territory here. These latent themes of rape are bolstered by overt, disturbing displays of actual sexual assault. The entity taking the form of Greg's mom violently assaulting her son is perhaps the most blatant, but the first time Jay sees the entity in her home, it's taken the form of a sexual assault victim. It's a young woman with a bruised face, her front teeth knocked out, and her arms secured behind her back. Her top is ripped, exposing one breast, and as she walks forwards she, the entity, stares blankly ahead. Amidst these manifest and latent portrayals and discussions of rape, the overall picture drives home the metaphor: Jay is battling a brutal, sexual injustice only she can see. Despite an exploration of a non-traditional (but no less horrifying) sexual assault, ultimately the result is the same: Jay's struggle is her own—apart from her loyal companions, she's surrounded by inept authorities and non-believers.

By challenging long-held arguments and assumptions used against the pervasiveness and authenticity of sexual assault, combined with a thorough exploration of teenage sexual anxiety, *It Follows* provides an examination, if indirectly so, of the intricacies of all aspects of the fears surrounding teen sexuality.

FOOTNOTES

1. Before the entity visits Jay in her home for the first time, we see a shot of Mrs. Height's legs and feet on the bed, with an empty wine glass next to a bottle. It does imply that she had a drink, but she's not stumbling around the hallway with a bottle of vodka in a death grip.

2. An earlier version of the script alludes to their mother having an active dating life. Early in the film, we're supposed to overhear Mrs. Height talking into the phone with a potential suitor, saying, 'Oh no I'd love to. That sounds fun. I could come over and cook for you if you'd like. I make a really delicious quiche. Do you like quiche?' Instead, her audio is all but inaudible, and a close listen betrays no hints about such a conversation.

3. There is one sort-of skyward shot not discussed here that occurs just after the group arrives at Greg's lake house. However, the shot only serves to establish nightfall, focuses on a tree trunk rather than the sky, and while the shot occurs outside everyone else is inside the house.

4. The script reveals that this subplot was to culminate with one of the boys stealing her undergarments, a move that was (obviously) dropped from the final film.

5. Here I'm discussing rape-revenge films where the victim is the one seeking vengeance on her attackers, thereby voiding such entries as *The Virgin Spring* (1960), *Last House on the Left* (1972), and the *Death Wish* franchise

6. In *Elle* (2016), Verhoeven does not have his heroine exact revenge even after learning the identity of her rapist, but this film is definitely an outlier, as she ultimately engages in a role-play rape fantasy with her attacker (who is ultimately killed by her son). But this complicated portrayal of an atypical reaction to sexual assault is a discussion for another time.

7. Here I use the term 'myth' not as an archetypal structure speaking to a larger society, but rather a smaller, case-specific sense more appropriately described as a ''misnomer.''

8. Stealthing is the act of removing a condom during intercourse without the partner's consent.

CHAPTER 5: 'I CAN'T DO THIS'

Few genres this side of rom-coms are as formulaic as horror. But, equally, this allows for a wide degree of subversion, which is a big part of horror's recent resurgence. With its unique threat, *It Follows* defies easy classification, but with its crop of teen characters (and unrelenting assailant), *It Follows* most closely falls into the slasher subgenre. With that comes a static group of victims, each falling into broad categories. There is purpose behind these relatively consistent portrayals, particularly as far as characters are concerned. These static templates offer a chance for subconscious audience participation, an almost-subliminal agreed upon shorthand for exposition:

> By establishing characters in extreme brief as broad, reductive, disreputable types (the snob, the asshole, the party hound, the slut, etc.), horror filmmakers can push viewers to do the hard work of filling in the blanks in thin characterizations—and, knowing that all of the characters may die, probably filling in those blanks from their own histories with obnoxious people. Slathering their own moral judgments over these simple, doomed avatars can give slasher fans a sense of catharsis—and make them feel more comfortable about being entertained by the characters' gory deaths. (Robinson, 2014)

Jay's entourage is not there to raise the body count—of the group, only Greg dies. On the contrary, these are sharply defined characters not lined up for execution, something rarely seen in ensemble horror films; even a recent classic like *The Descent* had its unique spelunkers systematically turned into crawler bait. This meaningful attention to each character represents an open universe approach to filmmaking:

> The idea of an open universe is the idea that pretty much anyone within the universe of that particular work of art could be at the center, and the work of art would still be interesting and well thought-out. The article argued that *Juno* [2007]…wasn't as open as *Knocked Up* [2007] because certain characters in it existed solely to either support or tear down the main character. They were ciphers, designed entirely to advance the story and the main character's arc. *Knocked Up*, meanwhile, had time for EVERYbody…It was egalitarian, where *Juno* was ruthlessly plotted. (VanDerWerff, 2011)

It's this open universe concept that provides depth to these characters, resulting in audience involvement that moves beyond spectatorship. The one attribute binding Kelly, Paul and Yara is concern at a level far beyond that we typically see. In *It Follows*, these three are quick to believe Jay, offering comfort, investigating a deserted house belonging to a potential rapist in the heart of Detroit, and escaping on an impromptu trip to an acquaintance's lake house, all of which occur before they see any form of physical evidence of the entity's existence.

Kelly has some small moments, like her walk home from work with her sister where we learn Kelly is still masking the fact that she smokes with a cherry ICEE; amusing given her mother's overall absence in the film. However, it's Yara's role that is especially intriguing. With the help of her shell phone, Yara plays an important role of the Greek chorus, but in contrast to this authoritative voice, she's the only one of her friends who is still behaving like someone who hasn't crossed the threshold into adolescence, leaving her largely impervious to the insanity happening around her. The first night the entity shows up at their house, Jay and Kelly are brushing their teeth to get ready for bed, cosmetics strewn over the counter: a nail file, moisturiser, and most notably contact solution—definitely not Yara's, who wears glasses throughout the film. Meanwhile Yara is sitting nearby clipping her toenails, and when she looks up a Red Vine is dangling out of her mouth. On the drive home from Hugh's, Kelly is comforting a dejected Jay, Greg is driving, Paul is staring quietly out the window…and Yara is passed out in the front, snoring, with potato chips strewn all over her lap and the seat. At the lake house, Yara's the only one swimming, paddling wobbly through the background in her pink inner tube while everyone else is sunbathing beneath a mostly overcast sky, and she's the only one wearing a one-piece swimsuit instead of a bikini.

Others are very aware of her physical development—namely Greg. When he is staring at her bare legs while she's standing on a countertop, she doesn't appear to notice, making her the only member of the group not acknowledging someone else's sexuality. The first scene at Greg's lake house, the camera tracks Yara as she shimmies through the house, loud music barely audible through her headphones as she steals a piece of bacon Kelly is preparing. This seeming obliviousness is amplified when compared with those surrounding her—Paul is pulling sheets off furniture, Greg is drinking a beer while nervously playing cards, and Jay is setting up a homemade alarm system on the window, mirroring Hugh's abandoned downtown home. Yara again fails to react to Greg's gaze, and not out of any apparent loyalty to Jay, but rather because she simply doesn't notice, or doesn't care.

All of this—the candy, the obliviousness, the innocence—further reinforces that Yara stands out because she is uniquely asexual in a film that, at its core, is about sex. Yara's lack of interest only highlights its importance. Horror films are no strangers to intercourse, but typically sex is rarely a prominent plot point and generally serves only to reinforce a character's archetype. Instead of sex as the subtext, the entire premise of It Follows hinges on a sexually transmitted curse. This emphasis on sex, combined with the fact that the characters in this film are conspicuously well-drawn for the genre, with each occupying a distinct space, allows the audience to watch another film occurring simultaneously within It Follows, a separate storyline running parallel to Jay's that mirrors another type of movie obsessed with intercourse: the coming of age subgenre.

The coming of age subgenre of teen films can fall into a number of categories, ranging from adventures in school to road trips. But one of the most prevalent subgenres is the teen romance, so popular that it often cuts across teen subgenres in the form of first dates, parties and prom. Regardless of setting, these films orbit around sex, particularly the rite of passage of losing one's virginity. This is because sex can signal adulthood, demonstrating 'a level of intimacy and responsibility' beyond their age, though with sex comes components such as 'senses of potency, obligation, and maturity' that these teens are not prepared to handle (Shary, 2014: 251). The boundary between being a virgin or non-virgin 'is not traversed in a single moment through a single act', but is rather a 'question of knowledge and experience rather than a physical transformation' (Tuck, 2010: 159). For movies, losing one's virginity is one of the ultimate rites of passage and an essential part of the coming-of-age journey captured on-screen. In the early 1980s, teens trying to lose their virginity was one of the most popular storylines, and it's one that has persisted, though in a slightly more evolved sense. Despite the madcap reputation of these films from the '80s, most later entries treat the actual decision of whether to have sex very seriously, creating surprisingly sombre moments against a potentially wacky plot.

With an emotionless murderer relentlessly pursuing Jay, the focus on sex is firmly fixed on her, and rightfully so. But a slight pivot reveals an identifiable coming-of-age structure as long as you focus (for the most part) on one of the other fascinating characters in the film: Paul. Mitchell argues Paul is worthy of attention:

> …he's someone who has grown up in this neighborhood. He's maybe just a little younger than Jay, and they were closer before. There's a point when you're kids and a year or two doesn't make a difference, and then there's a point when it does. This is that space. I like the idea of someone that has these feelings for her and is willing to do anything despite the fact that it's probably the worst idea on the planet. I think that's probably very much a teenage boy's reaction to having those kinds of feelings for someone—feeling separate from them, yet seeing this opportunity, as terrible as it is, to try to step into some type of role that he probably shouldn't. (Nastasi, 2015)

In our first scene with Paul, he's trying to act older and more mature than his two friends, clearly trying to impress Jay. At that moment, Yara farts, and Paul laughs, unable to help himself. The chuckling stops when he sees Jay leaving to go get ready for her date. It's obvious to everyone in the room that he's pining for her—even Yara openly scoffs. We see the challenge immediately: Paul needs to assert himself in a way that will allow Jay to consider him as a viable dating option. For Paul, the only (visible) obstacle is Greg, who plays the ex-boyfriend who dated Jay but 'should've been nicer' to her, an apparent lothario at ease surrounded by potential prospects. *It Follows* thankfully doesn't make Greg a caricature, which would only diminish Jay. Jay and Greg have history that grows out of shared classes, milestones, and experiences, giving him a built-in advantage. First and foremost, the two dated and slept together in high school, so there is a history behind every exchange. The two also reconnect through this bizarrely dangerous adventure. When Greg is showing Jay how to shoot a handgun, he tells Jay it's tough having to watch everyone else leave, clumsily attempting to discuss something other than the steadily approaching elephant in the room. Jay mumbles an agreement, but the question itself suggests a potentially powerful connection. Both were in the same classroom at nearby Wayne State University, suggesting everyone else in their graduating class moved away for college. There is no indication that Jay received poor grades in high school, and given the proximity of Greg's home to hers, and the fact that both have fathers who are (for whatever reason) no longer in the picture, it's likely both are in similar financial situations.

Yet, Greg is still the heel, a foil due his comeuppance. For one thing, despite taking everyone to the lake house and to Hugh's homes, he never truly believes Jay, something that becomes apparent when he talks with Kelly, Paul and Yara when Jay is not around. That mistrust is underscored by the shot of him eating with a table of young women in the union shortly after he slept with Jay, revealing that he has on the same outfit he wears to visit Jay in the hospital apparently later that same day.

Meanwhile, Paul plays a protagonist who occupies a unique space in the film. Like Greg, Jay and Paul also have a history, though in this case it's largely asexual. The closest they ever came to being involved was when they shared a first kiss years earlier…after which Paul immediately kissed her sister Kelly. Despite these challenges, Paul pines from afar, a lovelorn suitor too shy to approach. Paul is anything but a traditional alpha male. While Jay is learning to shoot a handgun, Yara, Kelly, and Paul are sitting on a blanket nearby; Yara is reading her e-book, Kelly is leaning back on both hands watching the target practice session and Paul is sitting cross-legged with both hands in his ears, clearly bothered by the volume of the gunshots. He's also prone to staring in anger/frustration/disbelief at Greg and Jay. Throughout *It Follows*, Paul is aware of what is happening, at least as far as those two are concerned. He stares at Greg comforting Jay during their trip to Hugh's high school, and Paul is back to staring into the room while Greg lightly rubs Jay's leg the day after they've had sex in her hospital bed.

The deck is clearly stacked against Paul, but the entire plot is surprisingly well-drawn, so he gets a real shot at his love interest. Scenes serve as romantic short stories before being rudely interrupted by a horror movie happening around them. When Paul stays over on the couch following Jay's encounter with the elderly stalker, he's up late, half-watching 1965's *Voyage to a Prehistoric Planet*, when Jay walks down the stairs to share in his insomnia. She sits at the other end of the couch, and they temporarily forget the threat walking steadily toward them. Every gesture becomes amplified; Jay slowly inches her feet closer to Paul's, she has her knees pulled up to her chest but her legs remain slightly apart as they reminisce about sharing their first kiss. Jay ribs him about also kissing Kelly, and the two remember in disbelief the time they found a dozen dirty magazines and the ensuing sex ed talk once adults found out. Paul seems to be minutes away from asking her out when a window breaks, and the entity staggers back into the picture.

Paul also believes Jay unquestioningly. After his quasi-romantic encounter on the couch is interrupted by shattering glass, he goes on a fruitless investigation, seeing nothing. Minutes later, when Kelly and Paul are trying to comfort a hysterical Jay, Yara knocks on the door. Despite seeing nothing downstairs, Paul grabs a broom and holds it like a baseball bat, ready to defend himself and Jay from something he has yet to see. Eventually, his faith is rewarded in an unfortunate way: when Paul sees Jay's hair being pulled by an invisible force, he breaks a beach chair against the entity and is violently knocked backward by it. He gets another shot at the entity in the natatorium.

During this final confrontation—when Paul finds the gun and rushes to save Jay—there is a moment when we see Paul finally get his chance to prove himself. Before leaving for the pool, Paul asks Jay why she chose to sleep with Greg instead of him. Jay reveals that she assumed Greg would be safe because he wasn't scared. Paul pushes for her to pass it on to him, but he is rebuffed; Jay is trying to protect him. However, Paul is hurt by the rejection, particularly since it is framed as him not being masculine enough to be anything more than her friend. However, the pool affords him the chance to prove himself, a chance for us (and Jay) to see the intersection of who he is and who he wants to be:

Paul's shadow depicts the hero he desperately wants to be.

Here we see Paul nervously holding the gun, his face locked in fear. Opposite his physical form is his shadow cast against the wall, arms locked in a classic action hero pose, the silhouette cool, determined and confident. He ends up playing a pivotal role in downing the entity, and he ultimately wins Jay's trust.

The director offers no clarification when talking about the first time Jay and Paul have sex: 'I do like that some people see it as them connecting in a kind of real way, and other people see it as a sad moment that's maybe one-sided' (Buchanan, 2015).

In another interview, Mitchell explains,

> I think Paul is very much in love with her. As for what her feelings are, I'm hesitant to say. Maybe I'm unveiling it here just in saying this, but I think that viewing things from a distance and the little bit of coldness and sadness, I think the camera contributes to that. It's always about keeping just enough space between the characters so that we can see the edges of the frame and the background. (Nastasi, 2015)

Even the ending of the film is drawn along gender lines, and it could easily become less about whether they are being followed by an entity and more about the emotional state of Jay and Paul. If Jay has 'settled' for Paul, it becomes a morality tale more overt than any '90s de-flowering plot or traditional slasher film. Ignoring the possibility of an entity in the background, the lesson here would still be incredibly depressing: If you survive, never have recreational sex outside of a stiflingly safe relationship. But if you look at the story through Paul's eyes, the nice guy finally finishes first; the woman he pined after for years is finally in love with him and won't ever leave.

But while Paul's storyline is an interesting diversion, it's nothing compared to the pressure placed on Jay, and not only in terms of keeping the beast at bay (the entity, not Paul). Even if she's able to stay one step ahead of the entity by not having sex with anyone else, virginity does not guarantee happily ever after, at least not in horror films. After all, plenty have derided the not-so-subtle lesson of the consequences of sexual desire for the female victims in horror films, but things don't necessarily turn out well for the virginal last-woman-standing either. The so-called lesson of slasher films and horror movies where the purest survive and the unclean are doomed to die young is one that is largely undone by sequels. In *Friday the 13th Part II* (1981), survivor Alice Hardy is murdered several weeks after surviving the Crystal Lake massacre. After losing her virginity mid-movie to Billy Loomis, *Scream*'s Sidney Prescott is tormented and traumatised for a decade. Laurie Strode survives for *twenty* years, never finding love or safety, eventually thrown from the roof of the sanitarium where she was institutionalised, by the killer who drove her insane.

This double-standard regarding sex and relationships in this film is best captured when Hugh is describing the dangers of the entity to Jay. He explains that she should find someone immediately and sleep with them. 'It should be easy for her, she's a girl. Any guy would be with you. Just sleep with somebody and tell them to do the same. Maybe it'll never come back.'

Thankfully, an important scene later in the film directly challenges this naïve statement. After seeing Greg fucked to death by his mother's doppelgänger, Jay drives for hours until she stops to sleep on her car in the woods, the fear of the entity overriding any hesitation about what lurks amidst the nighttime soundtrack of crickets and frogs. She awakens the next morning and hears the faint sound of music in the distance. She follows a path down to the lake where she sees three young men in a speedboat about 100 yards offshore. Without hesitation, she strips off her t-shirt and yoga pants, slowly wading into the water. It's clear that her plan is to sleep with at least one of those men. From a strictly logical standpoint, this is a no-brainer. On its face, evading the entity is a numbers game, and the more people you put between you and the entity increases the likelihood of them sleeping with others, which puts that many more degrees of separation between you. Again, logically speaking, she should swim out to the boat, have sex with all three if possible, swim back to the car, and be ready to find the next potential person to pass this along to if one of the guys from the boat succumbs to the entity.

Yet, this scenario presupposes a lot of things; namely, that these men *want* to have sex with her. They might be gay. They might be in committed relationships. They may be in gay, committed relationships. Hell, they just might not want to. Any number of contextual reasons as to why a woman wouldn't want to have sex with a man are cast aside to perpetuate this myth of instant sexual gratification for women if they so desire; the next step in this bizarre line of thought is that women who are unhappy have only themselves to blame. This mindset also assumes that Jay doesn't care about the fact that she would be sentencing these men to death, which again says a lot more about the Hughs of the world than the Jays.

As for whether Jay actually made it out to the boat for sex, we never really find out. Driving home with a dejected look on her face might signal dismay at what she'd done, or it might be her possibly wondering why she couldn't go through with it. Again, Mitchell's vague, contradictory cues to denote the passage of time distort the timeline. Jay is still wearing the same shirt that she wore on the drive home from her encounter at the lake. Given that she's wearing the same shirt even though she never repeats an outfit the rest of the film, and that the broken window at Greg's house is still covered up with plywood, an argument can be made that she never slept with the boys on the boat. An earlier script is less subtle and outright shows her not going through with it:

> Jay takes off her pants and shirt as she steps into the lake. She moves out, bracing herself against the cold – letting her cast drop carelessly into the water. She swims further. The boat is ahead. The young men grow closer and closer. Jay slows and stops. She's near the boat now. The music and laughter is louder. She looks up at the figures of men - considering. She starts to call out, but stops… She starts to call out, but stops. Her eyes show melancholy as she paddles in place. I can't do this.

'I can't do this.' In a simple four-word phrase, Jay makes a bold decision with potentially dire consequences. This course of action would be a bold, blatant stance for asserting independence, the moment in the film when Jay decides she's not going to be manipulated by the entity any longer. It would make for a definite turning point in any horror film marking a shift from victim to victor, only we don't know for certain if that's what she actually decides to do. This ambivalence is, in essence, what the film is using to counter Hugh's ignorant claim regarding how much easier it would be for her than him, all through the lens of the horror film structure.

The decision to have sex—and live (albeit uncertainly) with the consequences of that decision create a gendered interpretation of dealing with the entity, one we see reflected through subtle use of the colour palette throughout the film. What's particularly damning is Mitchell's use of hues—in particular, the colour pink—as indicators for Jay's mentality. The most feminine of colours, it's used throughout the majority of the film to underscore Jay's mindset, particularly toward the issue of the entity. The first shot we see of Jay, she's wearing a black one-piece bathing suit, suggesting a bold, asexual heroine. However, moments after she moves indoors, when Jay is getting ready for her movie date with Hugh, her image is drastically softened. The window bathes half of her bedroom in a soft, white light, accentuating and enhancing the pink highlights: the pink flowers on her curtains, the pink comforter and pillowcase, her pink dress. However, the other, less-lit half of the room is the tonal opposite: dark teal walls. The only light source here is Jay's red and yellow flower lamp, the two colours fusing together to mirror the rose-pink display on the far side of the room.

Jay sits on her bed, bathed in warm light from the window and her unique dresser lamp.

This establishes Jay as overtly feminine, a trait only reinforced when, on their following date, she's wearing a matching pink bra and underwear set; as she planned on having sex with him on that date, the undergarment choice was a form of performance, of reinforcing her gendered identity.

Following Hugh's assault on Jay, the colour pink largely disappears from the film, apart from two significant moments, both taking place on a beach. The first is at the lake house, when Jay has slowly been reconnecting with Greg. Beneath her navy blue, partially zipped hoodie, we see a bright pink bikini top poking through, a fleeting glimpse of her femininity ready to reassert itself. In fact, Jay is getting ready to remove her jacket to get in the water when she's attacked by the entity. The last vestige of pink we see is when she sheds layers to swim out to the boat, in which she reveals a pink tank top, followed by neon pink underwear so bright it almost makes her top look orange. Rather than the innocence of the preparation for her first date, this feels like a costume she (unconvincingly) dons to win over her potential partner(s).

After we see Jay driving back from standing on the shore staring at the boat, she's back in her room and the camera slowly pans across her bed. The pink comforter is still there, but it's obscured by a dark blue carpeting and pillowcase, by Kelly's grey sweater and blue undershirt, and by Yara's blue pants. Lying next to the bed and not on the comforter is Jay, her head on a blue patchwork pillow with a blue image on her white t-shirt. The camera pulls in tight on Jay, her skin and t-shirt bathed in thin blue sheen reflecting off the navy bed sheet. Paul knocks on the door and we get a wide shot of the room, this time from the floor-level. While we still see glimpses of pink from the first glimpse of her room, it's definitely a tonal shift.

The same room seen in a different light evokes a darker, more sombre tone.

Hugh's approach of simply 'passing it along to someone else' denotes his mindset—a male mindset—echoing the deception he used to affix the entity to Jay. Yet even this bold use of colour remains ambiguous. The colour scheme could suggest that, despite what the script may have originally called for, Jay *did* sleep with at least one of the guys on the boat. This would suggest she has bought in to Hugh's 'solution' for defeating the entity, which is ultimately no solution at all—a dominant, sexual approach that clearly has not worked in the past. At the same time, the blue hue could also signify the aforementioned independence from her pink existence, a break from gender norms.

Ultimately, in the horror universe, it's not 'easier' because Jay's a girl. In fact, due to a recent trend in the genre, she might have it tougher than ever before. Spanning the better part of a century, it's difficult to make a sweeping statement about any genre; any misstep can be countered with an exception, be it an individual film or an entire subgenre. That said, speaking broadly, horror genre has a long, problematic history with women. With its mainstream popularity fused with the male gaze, these issues are overt, as the uniqueness of the horror film raises the stakes for overt displays of misogyny. Unlike other genres, the gender issues become more pronounced because there's a far greater likelihood of death and dismemberment in a scary movie than, say, a romantic comedy. It's this fusion of murder and torture with intercourse that raises blood-red flags.

Not everyone agrees with this reputation, of course. When discussing It Follows, Mitchell scoffed at the idea, saying, 'We've sort of accepted this other academic read as a pop culture fact. I would question that just because we've heard it in Scream or read the books it comes from, doesn't necessarily mean it's fact.' Likely referring to Sidney Prescott's, 'Some stupid killer stalking some big-breasted girl who can't act who is always running up the stairs when she should be running out the front door' commentary, Mitchell isn't wrong. The genre has come a long way from its depiction of hapless, helpless female victims thanks to evolved, emboldened female protagonists.[1] But in some ways—and in particular in some subgenres—the sexism is embedded in its DNA, an outdated programming flaw, the very design of which contributed to its success during a less sophisticated time. Despite the awareness of these problems to the point of satire, sexualisation (and ensuing punishment for said sexualisation) is still prevalent. Andrew Welsh's systematic content analysis of the last 40 years of horror films found that women who had sex in these movies were significantly less likely to survive and had significantly longer death scenes than their chaste counterparts (Welsh, 2010). He also found that women who had sex in the films were more likely to be killed than the men they were sleeping with, a double standard with particularly high stakes.[2]

One of the broadest stock characters for the horror film is one whose gendered portrayal receives plenty of attention: the Final Girl. Carol Clover identified the Final Girl as a young woman introduced as a main character who survives (finding the bodies of her friends along the way) to be the last person standing in order to do battle with the villain. She's clearly identified as the main character from the outset and is normally gifted with a talent or occupation that sets her apart from the walking dead in her group. She's either a virgin (Laurie in Halloween) or sexually unavailable (Stretch in Texas Chain Saw Massacre), which is why she is 'rewarded' with survival. She's smart, observant, and calm, 'the first character to sense something amiss and the only one to deduce from the accumulating evidence the pattern and extent of the threat' (Clover, 1992: 44).[3] This concept was established in the heart of the slasher film, but has extended far beyond that subgenre's heyday. Clover's canonic discussion of this character is a prescient one, as it serves as an important mile-marker, something common enough to be routinely observed—particularly as a horror movie character staple—but ideally evolving enough to see some difference.

As per Clover's criteria, at first glance, Jay makes for a convincing Final Girl. She is undoubtedly the main character of the film, the first to appear after Annie's demise and clearly central to the plot. Beyond that, the similarities fade quickly. She's particularly relatable because she does *not* have a unique set of skills or employment history. She's not a virgin and breaks the clichéd taboo of having sex during the movie. She's intelligent but not the brainiac Laurie Strode appears to be. She's observant out of necessity (as no one else can warn her of the danger), and she's understandably anything but calm, at least until she finds a trustworthy companion. Moreover, she definitely doesn't watch her friends get picked off one by one until she does something about it. The characteristics don't fit because that's not her character. Like the genre, Jay has moved beyond the Final Girl assignment to achieve a new identity, the latest adaptation of horror evolution, and one rarely seen in US horror films: the Only Girl.[4]

Plenty of horror films feature a female protagonist battling the enemy on her own after the deaths of her companions, but the Camping Trip Massacre format has steadily declined in favour of smaller casts. In the process, more films featured an ill-fated couple encountering random acts of violence. A sort-of Final Girl emerges in this format, with the male partner ultimately incapacitated, be it the predictable *Vacancy* (2007) or the unsettling *Eden Lake* (2008). But the Only Girl is a very recent addition to the horror canon. We see the first glimpses of this phenomenon in reverse with *Psycho* (1960), though it falls apart once Norman intervenes. In the well-constructed 1967 thriller *Wait Until Dark*, we see glimpses of the Only Girl in Audrey Hepburn's Oscar-nominated performance as a blind woman tormented in her apartment by three men searching for a doll filled with heroin. It's not a perfect example: Hepburn is assisted through the film by a teen girl on its periphery, and Hepburn is only in imminent danger for the final third of the film. Still, she's largely on her own, rather than part of a group of people who are threatened and then systematically killed off. Eleven years later, Camille Keaton starred in *I Spit on Your Grave* (1978), a nasty, exploitive film with substantially less cachet and substantially more vengeful castration than Hepburn's contribution. Keaton plays a writer who seeks the solitude of secluded cabin to pen her first novel. Four locals brutally rape her in some of the most disturbing scenes this side of *Irreversible* (2002), after which she exacts her revenge. In the last few years, we've seen a resurgence of horror movies featuring a lone woman protagonist: *Hush* (2016), *Kristy* (2014), *Curve* (2015), and *House of the Devil* (2009), with others, such as *The Babadook* (2014), that might also qualify.

The Only Girl is not to be confused with simply having a female protagonist acting on her own. For instance, in *The Silence of the Lambs* (1991), Jodi Foster is largely stalking the killer rather than being hunted, plus she has the temporary assistance of Dr. Lecter; if the film broke off and followed Precious the dog instead, she's probably closer to the Only Girl than Foster.

The Only Girl is alone once the threat is realised and remains so for the rest of the movie—apart from the killer, of course. The entire point of Clover's original concept of the Final Girl is that the killer slashed his way through everyone else, leaving her to fend for herself. For the Only Girl, this is largely done through physical isolation. In *Hush*, Kate Siegel is a deaf writer who only lives near one person in walking distance. *Kristy* takes place on a small college campus, but literally every other student has left for Thanksgiving. The Only Girl is on her own for most of the film—others might briefly drift into the killer's periphery to underscore the gravity of the threat, but they play a relatively minor role and are dispatched almost as quickly as they appear. They do not discuss the threat with her and mostly appear at the beginning of the film for character development and exposition. Most importantly, they do not realise or acknowledge there is a danger until it's too late. Michael Trucco is stabbed in the neck and bleeds out in *Hush* after being on-screen less than seven minutes. Greta Gerwig is shot in the head while lighting her cigarette in the criminally underseen *House of the Devil*. These deaths aren't preceded by a substantial contribution in terms of adding insight to the killer's motive, nor do they provide the key to defeating evil incarnate.

Sex also has nothing to do with it. The Final Girl's oft-discussed virginal status has evolved a bit, to the point of being playfully mocked in *Behind the Mask: The Rise of Leslie Vernon* and *The Cabin in the Woods*. But the Only Girl is not celibate, as she's typically in either a serious relationship or just getting out of one. Simply put, her sexuality is mentioned but doesn't serve as a motivating principle or character arc. Indeed, the only hint we have of Jay's sexual past is before the final act of the film, and even then we only learn of it because Jay is trying to explain to Paul why she chose Greg over him. Justine has a serious boyfriend (at least for a while) in *Kristy*, and Samantha is surprisingly, refreshingly asexual in *House of the Devil*.

What's particularly fascinating about the Only Girl phenomenon is the male equivalent: namely, that there isn't one. The action-adventure genre likely wouldn't exist without men going rogue, but that never really extended to the horror genre. Lone males do most of the heavy lifting as far as murderers and psychopaths in horror films, but outside of that, they are not asked to carry a film in this manner. The closest a male protagonist usually gets to a showdown is usually being when it's reduced to the aforementioned couple, and even then he's usually left for dead (*Eden Lake*) or outright killed (*Backcountry*). Even in the rare instance when he makes to the final battle, it's to rescue the damsel in distress.

What makes *It Follows* so unique in this regard is that Mitchell manages to paradoxically have an Only Girl surrounded by people. Through his innovative use of the unseen entity, Mitchell manages to largely create an Only Girl scenario for someone who is surrounded by friends and lives in a major city. But the components are there. At no point are Jay's family or friends in danger, only Jay herself. Once the entity kills Jay, it's not going to come after Kelly or Jay's mom or the rest of the neighbourhood. Jay's focus on her own safety isn't selfish, it's survival, but what's unique is that there are no larger stakes. Sci-fi/horror films almost always allude to a larger threat—the takeover of a city, a country, or the world by some external threat if it's not stopped immediately. Even when the threat doesn't extend beyond the city limits, there are still stakes involved; Laurie Strode was protecting the kids she was babysitting as much as she was fighting for her own life. And while Jay's friends stick with her, Jay remains isolated for significant portions of the film, realising that the burden was ultimately hers.

The Only Girl is an essential next step in the portrayal of women in horror films, not only because it disrupts the rigid, gendered hierarchy but also because any genre should evolve/adapt to societal cues in order to best reflect the broader cultural conversation. The Only Girl phenomenon captures the current zeitgeist of female empowerment, and it's remarkably unique in that there is no male equivalent for this, at least not in this genre. Horror films may have taken a significant step forward, but, as demonstrated with Jay's struggle in terms of dealing with the entity, the nuances that accompany this change might carry unexpected baggage, potentially shackled by horror conventions long-since engrained in the genre. In other words, depending on how the light streams through the window, the room might just as easily still be pink.

FOOTNOTES

1. I'm looking—nay *staring*—at you, *The Descent*.
2. Welsh's study is not without its flaws, most notably that it's difficult to establish a quantitative coding guide for specific types of sexual activity. However, his is the first (and, at the time of this publication, only) research study to examine how frequently these tropes about sex in horror films actually occurred.
3. In the least-convincing aspect of Clover's argument, she suggests that another indicator of how the Final Girl is allied with her male counterparts is through her male name (e.g. Stevie, Marti, Terry, Laurie). While this is a bit of a stretch, here it works: Jay.
4. The use of 'girl' describing adult women is admittedly problematic, but in the interest of consistency—not to mention in homage to Clover—I'll continue the use of 'girl' when discussing this phenomenon.

CHAPTER 6: PATH TO VICTORY

The final scene of *It Follows* is deliberately vague, as Paul and Jay walk down a sidewalk, chastely holding hands as they tap out a secret code to one another. Behind them, wearing a white t-shirt, a blurry figure follows them, though Mitchell playfully has the person wearing a heavy, dark jacket over it to keep things somewhat ambiguous, as we've previously seen the entity dressed in white (or nude). Whether they're actually being followed or if they're free from the entity forever remains a mystery; credits roll before the person behind them can get any closer. Some have pointed to Paul's shot to the top of the entity's head in the pool—and the ensuing blood-red water—as the end of the entity, a breaking of the curse. However, in the previous scene, Yara was reading Dostoyevsky aloud in the hospital bed: 'The most terrible agony may not be in the wounds themselves but in knowing for certain that within an hour, then within ten minutes, then within half a minute, now at this very instant – your soul will leave your body and you will no longer be a person, and that this is certain; the worst thing is that *it is certain*' (emphasis added). Perhaps the two know this and are preparing to fight it together. Then again, perhaps Jay and Paul have learned to live with the chase, understanding that sharing the struggle is more important than the threat itself. While playing Old Maid on the porch, Yara has earlier read another excerpt aloud from Dostoyevsky off of her shell phone:

> I think that if one is faced by inevitable destruction – if a house is falling upon you, for instance – one must feel a great longing to sit down, close one's eyes and wait, come what may.

This is the ultimate conclusion for whomever is tethered to the entity. We see it at the beginning of the film quite literally: Annie sitting on the ground, back to the water, with her brake lights blanketing the woods from which her brutal destruction will emerge. She has accepted her fate, calling her parents for a formal goodbye and waiting for the entity's inevitable arrival. As long as Jay and Paul keep walking, they have a chance.

Regardless of how (or if) they've ultimately managed to cope, the question that remains is how you kill the entity. To put it kindly, Paul's plan wasn't it. His idea in the third act is not only unsuccessful (it's a bullet to the top of the head, not a hair dryer, that stopped the entity), it's wildly ill-advised. Even his director agreed. Mitchell stated,

> It's the stupidest plan ever! It's a kid-movie plan, it's something that Scooby-Doo
> and the gang might think of and that was sort of the point. What would you do if
> you were confronted by a monster and found yourself trapped within a nightmare?
> Ultimately, you would have to resort to some way of fighting it that's accessible to
> you in the physical world, and that's not really going to cut it…they do their best to
> accomplish something and we witness its failure. (Buchanan, 2015)

On the surface, defeating the entity has several potential solutions, if only because the
movie avoids providing too many details. The ocean might be a barrier, though *Zombi 2*
(1979) and *Land of the Dead* showed zombies undeterred by a walk in the ocean, sharks
be damned. Mountains would theoretically provide a formidable obstacle, but the first
time we see the entity, it is at the bottom of a steep embankment, and seconds later,
it's on the floor of the building, continuing its endless walkathon. Given the limitations
grounded in its zombie/slasher identity, it's unlikely that the entity would materialise,
fly, or even scramble around a mountain chain, but it doesn't seem like it would be
slowed. That said, the brilliance of the entity is that its origins and powers are never truly
explored. It's entirely possible that the entity does possess the ability to move through
obstacles (at a walking pace) until it gets within close proximity to its target; this would
explain how we occasionally first see the entity standing in front of a wall or building
with no visible means of exit.

A flight to Chile, Norway or Fiji would provide a respite, but only if you kept a certain
amount of distance between you and the entity; to borrow a phrase from Truman
Burbank: 'You can't get any further away until you start coming back'. In other words,
if physical barriers were an effective means at slowing the entity, putting the Mariana
Trench between you and it might seem like a sound strategy; but the earth is round, so
the entity could just as easily walk the other direction. A foreign country might not be
the best option either. Your surroundings would be alien, and *everything* would likely be
suspicious. In a space where everything seems new and unusual, your ability to detect
something inherently different would be difficult. As previously discussed, the entity is
cunning in how it alters its appearance, so it likely wouldn't appear as a friend or relative,
opting instead for a stranger amongst a crowd of strangers. Moreover, jet-setting across

the globe every 1-2 weeks is difficult to do without being independently wealthy, as a job under such circumstances would be difficult to maintain.

At this point I've raved enough about Mitchell's concept of the entity that I might as well be Mitchell himself (or at least the entity pretending to be him), but it bears repeating that his creation is savvy, particularly because it exists during a time when discussions of sex, particularly for teens, is difficult. Parents think their kids aren't old enough or are simply uneasy with the subject matter, and teens often lack either the motivation or initiative for such an uncomfortable conversation. It's because of these complications that the entity is able to thrive, which is why the best solution isn't barriers, distance, or a steady diet of orgies. The best solution is communication.

Teens talk. Like, a lot. And this is reflected in horror films featuring adolescents in one of three ways. The first is practical and immediate: interpersonal communication. This is the most straightforward and the most obvious, and it involves other characters directly. They're friends (or at least acquaintances sharing in a struggle), and so discussing their thoughts and observations is a natural response to a threat. The second is technological: the news media. Use of the media grounds the film in the real world. Whether it's the newspaper headlines in *Night of the Demon* (1957) or the intermittent radio and TV news updates in *Night of the Living Dead*, these reports tend to serve as the Greek chorus for horror films, a way of tethering the experiences of a small group to what's happening in the rest of the world while occasionally providing important information for defeating the threat. Heavier media involvement can also shape the film in different ways. The reporter herself can also serve as a catalyst for moving the story along. By inserting Gale Weathers and her coverage of the Woodsboro murders into the *Scream* franchise, it provides a chance to hear what authorities think of the case, the prime suspects, and general progress in catching a killer.

The final is mystical: urban legend. These tireless retellings of local phenomenon are practically supernatural themselves in that no one asks how everyone knows the Myers house is haunted or questions how future generations learned of Leslie Vernon's survival; they just *know*. Stubbersfield and colleagues defined urban legends as 'apocryphal stories, which are told as true, involve an urban or suburban setting, and feature a single event, usually an individual experience, as the core of the narrative'

(2015: 291). An urban legend is first and foremost a story; each has exposition, an inciting incident, climax and denouement. But in weaving a tale, S. Elizabeth Bird argues that through the urban legend 'certain narratives become salient' and that salience 'is enmeshed in the fears, concerns, even pleasures of a particular cultural moment' (1996: 147). In other words, while an urban legend is, by definition, untrue, it retains a cultural resonance which assists in its rapid transmission. The moral of the story can be overt ('Welcome to the world of AIDS') or latent (subtle messages about a rescued dog actually being a rat from Mexico or Haiti), but it must be present.

The first two modes of discussion are pretty straightforward. Out of necessity, It Follows has interpersonal communication; Jay (and the audience) must be told some basic rules. Without Hugh's rundown on the entity's existence, form, and motivation, Jay likely wouldn't make it out of her classroom. The absence of media reports is surprising. This could easily be a desire for Mitchell to mask the time period of the film; each of the movies being shown in the background were released between 1954 and 1965, yet they're broadcast on newer cathode ray tube sets. Yara uses her shell phone, but only to read aloud Dostoyevsky excerpts.[1]

But most surprising of all is the absence of the urban legend; the girl who slept around and was found brutally murdered by the lake, or the boy who lures women to their inevitable doom. The film itself is tailor-made for such a tale—critic Drew McWeeny even gushed that 'It Follows feels like an urban legend you've known your whole life' (2014). In It Follows, it's in the best interest of the entity not to have people aware of the potential danger, as it could cut down on potential targets. And even if people are actively refuting the story, but the more vociferously one attacks the allegations, the more real the conspiracy sounds. Mitchell understandably wanted to distance himself from having the entire film reduced to an allegory about STDs, but the plot itself is surprisingly reminiscent of a particularly resilient urban legend that made the national news in 1991. The story was about a woman so bitter about the fact that she had contracted HIV that she was going to nightclubs to sleep with men so that she wouldn't be the only one to die alone. Elizabeth Bird reminds us that news, like urban legends, is a cultural construction, and so the story was covered breathlessly in the news media until eventually learning it was a hoax. But it went viral (well, '90s-viral) because it resonated so much with audiences and journalists; AIDS was seen as a terrifying new plague and the story placed a villainous face on the disease to ground it. But one of the key details to this piece was that the perpetrator was a woman, serving as a cautionary tale for men who must avoid a gorgeous temptress but also doubling as the 'embodiment of a just reward—like many legends, she demonstrates that immoral behaviour will be punished horribly and disproportionately' (Bird, 2003: 153).

This is Hugh's description of how he ended up targeted by the entity: 'I met a girl at a bar. It was a one night stand... I don't even know her name. I think that's where it came from.' This story is tailor-made for an urban legend. It's simple, carries a moral message, and is vague enough to allow for the storyteller to add pertinent details. Within the context of the horror genre, the urban legend is surprisingly useful, a warning about a local threat. Hugh's impromptu lesson is detailed and succinct out of necessity—his survival depends on it. But the story of the entity is one that demands a whisper campaign about strange disappearances or someone insisting they were being followed. The collective memory of a specific geographic area, along with the imagined community understood by those who share the legend, should result in this cautionary tale reaching nationwide teen saturation in a matter of weeks.

And so the trick to defeating the entity is not building a seemingly impenetrable fortress or flying around the globe, but rather a much more cost effective solution of talking openly about the threat. Picture a social network where an open, ongoing conversation existed tracking the entity through a record of sexual contact. Void of boasting, judgement, or (hopefully) reviews, the users could track the entity through simply warning others. Every time someone was about to travel, they could let that next community know and see if the population could shoulder the burden for a while. The massive means available online would keep the beast at bay. Mapping apps would track its speed, photos and police reports would document existing cases to non-believers, Kickstarter would finance putting some distance between a community and the entity... the possibilities are endless. But this starts with a healthy, honest conversation about partners in a tolerant, sex-positive society, and until that happens, the entity will continue to roam. At this rate, it's probably going to be walking for quite some time.

FOOTNOTES

1. When Greg tries to visit Jay (just before his demise), the script states that Kelly and Paul are talking and listening to music on the porch while 'Yara is chatting with someone on her pink cell phone'. However, this is not apparent in the film.

REFERENCES

Ancuta, Katarzyna. 'Ringu and the vortex of horror: contemporary Japanese horror and the technology of chaos.' *Asian Journal of Literature, Culture and Society* 1 (2015): 23-42.

Anderson, Kyle. "'It Follows": The Story Behind DIsasterpeace's Score.' *Entertainment Weekly*, 20, Dec. 2016, http://ew.com/article/2015/03/27/it-follows-score/. Accessed 21 April 2017.

Barone, Matt. 'Horror-movie Music is Coming Back from the Dead.' *The Dissolve*, 12 Mar. 2015. https://thedissolve.com/features/exposition/955-horror-movie-music-is-coming-back-from-the-dead/. Accessed 22 April 2017.

Benedict, Helen. *Virgin or vamp: How the press covers sex crimes*. New York: Oxford University, 1993.

Berry, Brian JL. 'Islands of renewal in seas of decay.' *The new urban reality* (1985): 69-96.

Bird, S. Elizabeth. 'CJ's revenge: Media, folklore, and the cultural construction of AIDS.' *Critical Studies in Media Communication* 13.1 (1996): 44-58.

Bishop, Kyle William. *American Zombie Gothic: The Rise and Fall (and Rise) of the Walking Dead in Popular Culture*. North Carolina: McFarland & Company, 2010.

Bruni, Frank. 'The Spirit and Promise of Detroit.' *The New York Times*, 9 Sep. 2015. https://www.nytimes.com/2015/09/09/opinion/frank-bruni-the-spirit-and-promise-of-detroit.html. Accessed 28 May 2017.

Buchanan, Kyle. 'It Follows Spoiler Bomb: The Director Explains All Those Twists and Shocks.' *Vulture*, 27, Mar. 2015. http://www.vulture.com/2015/03/it-follows-director-the-spoiler-interview.html. Accessed 25 May 2017.

Buder, Emily. '5 Reasons "It Follows" Became the Surprise Indie Hit of the Year.' *IndieWire*, 29, September 2015, http://www.indiewire.com/2015/09/5-reasons-it-follows-became-the-surprise-indie-hit-of-the-year-57345/. Accessed 12 February 2017.

Clover, Carol J. *Men, Women, and Chainsaws: Gender in the modern horror film*. New Jersey: Princeton University Press, 1992/2015.

Cruchiola, Jordan. 'What Makes the New Horror Film It Follows So Damn Good.' *Wired*, 17, Mar. 2015, https://www.wired.com/2015/03/it-follows-unholy-trinity/. Accessed 16 January 2017.

Crump, Andy. 'The Feeling of Following: An Interview with David Robert Mitchell.' *Paste Magazine*, 17, Mar. 2015. https://www.pastemagazine.com/articles/2015/03/the-feeling-of-following-an-interview-with-david-r.html. Accessed 14 May 2017.

Denson, Shane, and Julia Leyda, eds. *Post-Cinema: Theorizing 21st-Century Film*. Sussex: REFRAME Books, 2016.

Dowd, A.A. 'David Robert Mitchell on His Striking New Horror Film, *It Follows*.' *AV Club*, 12, Mar. 2015. http://www.avclub.com/article/david-robert-mitchell-his-striking-new-horror-film-216215. Accessed 25 April 2017.

Fear, David. '"It Follows": The Story Behind the Year's Creepiest Film.' *Rolling Stone*, 12, Mar. 2015. http://www.rollingstone.com/movies/features/it-follows-the-story-behind-the-years-creepiest-film-20150312. Accessed 21 January 2017.

Flores, Linda A. 'Dynamic Rhetorics of Race: California's Racial Privacy Initiative and the Shifting Grounds of Racial Politics.' *Communication and Critical/Cultural Studies*, vol. 3, no. 3, 2006, pp. 181-201.

Florida, Richard. 'Class-Divided Cities: Detroit Edition.' *Citylab*, 10 Apr. 2013. https://www.citylab.com/equity/2013/04/class-divided-cities-detroit-edition/4679/. Accessed 24 May 2017.

Forcen, Fernando Espi. *Monsters, Demons, and Psychopaths: Psychiatry and Horror Film*. Boca Raton, Florida: CRC Press, 2017.

Giroux, Henry A. 'Racial Politics and the Pedagogy of Whiteness.' *Whitenesss: A Critical Reader*, edited by Mike Hill, 294-315. New York: New York University Press, 1997.

Hunter, Rob. '18 Things We Learned from the It Follows Commentary.' *Film School Rejects*, 13, Jul. 2015. https://filmschoolrejects.com/18-things-we-learned-from-the-it-follows-commentary-3a4c39261ceb/. Accessed 12 April 2017.

Jackson, Kimberly. *Gender and the Nuclear Family in Twenty-First-Century Horror*. New York: Palgrave Macmillan, 2016.

Kelly, Casey Ryan. 'Camp Horror and the Gendered Politics of Screen Violence: Subverting the Monstrous-Feminine in Teeth (2007).' *Women's Studies in Communication* 39.1 (2016): 86-106.

Kendrick, James. 'Slasher Films and Gore in the 1980s.' In *A Companion to the Horror Film*, edited by Harry M. Benshoff, 310-328. John Wiley & Sons, 2017.

Kirk, Jeremy. 'Interview: Director David Robert Mitchell on Nightmares + "It Follows."' *FirstShowing.Net*, 3 Apr. 2015. http://www.firstshowing.net/2015/interview-director-david-robert-mitchell-on-nightmares-it-follows/. Accessed 4 February 2017.

Leyda, Julia. 'Demon debt: Paranormal activity as recessionary post-cinematic allegory.' *Jump Cut* 56 (2014): 2014-2015.

Luckhurst, Roger. Zombies: *A Cultural History*.London: Reaktion Books, 2015.

McWeeny, Drew. 'Review: "It Follows" Offers Up Some Fresh Horror Ideas from a Rising Indie Filmmaking Star.' *Hitfix*, 18, May 2014. http://uproxx.com/hitfix/review-it-follows-offers-up-some-fresh-horror-ideas-from-a-rising-indie-filmmaking-star/. Accessed 21 January 2017.

Meyers, Jeff. 'Detroit-made "It Follows" Gives the Horror Genre a Much-Needed Jolt.' *Detroit Metro Times*, 25, Mar. 2015, http://www.metrotimes.com/detroit/detroit-made-it-follows-gives-the-horror-genre-a-much-needed-jolt/Content?oid=2316882. Accessed 22 April 2017.

Morrow, Brendan. '"It Follows" is Not About STDs. It's About Life As a Sexual Assault Survivor.' *Bloody Disgusting*, 27, Apr. 2016, http://bloody-http://flavorwire.com/509639/a-hint-of-joy-before-it-all-goes-to-hell-it-follows-director-david-robert-mitchell-on-teen-sex-horror-and-the-virgin-tropedisgusting.com/editorials/3387893/follows-not-stds-life-sexual-assault-survivor/. Accessed 15 May 2017.

Murphy, Mekado. 'David Robert Mitchell Narrates a Scene from "It Follows."' *New York Times*, 5 Mar. 2015. https://artsbeat.blogs.nytimes.com/2015/03/05/david-robert-mitchell-narrates-a-scene-from-it-follows/. Accessed 7 May 2017.

Nastasi, Alison. '"A Hint of Joy Before It All Goes to Hell": "It Follows" Director David Robert Mitchell on Teen Sex, Horror, and the Virgin Trope.' *Flavorwire*, 16, Mar. 2015, http://flavorwire.com/509639/a-hint-of-joy-before-it-all-goes-to-hell-it-follows-director-david-robert-mitchell-on-teen-sex-horror-and-the-virgin-trope. Accessed 27 March 2017.

Nemiroff, Perri. 'David Robert Mitchell Talks IT FOLLOWS, His Original Nightmare, the IT and More.' *Collider*, 10, Mar. 2015. http://collider.com/david-robert-mitchell-it-follows-interview/. Accessed 14 May 2017.

Odell, Colin, and Michelle LeBlanc. *Horror Films*. Harpenden: Oldcastle Books, 2010.

Pegg, Simon. 'The Dead and the Quick.' *The Guardian*, 3, November 2008. https://www.theguardian.com/media/2008/nov/04/television-simon-pegg-dead-set. Accessed 22 June May 2017.

Reese, Laura A., Jeanette Eckert, Gary Sands, and Igor Vojnovic. '"It's Safe to Come, We've Got Lattes": Development Disparities in Detroit.' *Cities* 60 (2017): 367-377.

Robinson, Tasha. 'Keynote: The Multi-Level Stereotypes of The Cabin in the Woods.' *The Dissolve*, 31, Mar. 2014, https://thedissolve.com/features/movie-of-the-week/490-keynote-the-multi-level-stereotypes-of-the-cabin-i/. Accessed 9 December 2016.

Shary, Timothy. *Generation Multiplex: The Image of Youth in American Cinema Since 1980*. Austin: University of Texas Press, 2014.

Simon, Barbara Levy. *Never Married Women*. Philadelphia: Temple University Press, 1987.

Sipos, Thomas M. *Horror Film Aesthetics: Creating the Visual Language of Fear*. North Carolina: McFarland & Company, 2010.

Smith, Grady. '"The Myth of the American Sleepover" Trailer.' *Entertainment Weekly*, 6 Jul. 2011. http://ew.com/article/2011/07/06/the-myth-of-the-american-sleepover-trailer/. Accessed 12 June 2017.

Stubbersfield, Joseph M., Jamshid J. Tehrani, and Emma G. Flynn. 'Serial killers, spiders and cybersex: Social and survival information bias in the transmission of urban legends.' *British Journal of Psychology* 106.2 (2015): 288-307.

Tudor, Andrew. 'Monsters and mad scientists.' *Genre* 1 (1989): 1931-1960.

VanDerWerff, Todd. 'Community: For a Few Paintballs More.' *A.V. Club*, 12 May, 2011. http://www.avclub.com/tvclub/community-for-a-few-paintballs-more-55900

Welsh, Andrew. 'On the perils of living dangerously in the slasher horror film: Gender differences in the association between sexual activity and survival.' *Sex Roles* 62.11-12 (2010): 762-773.